Roots & Water

Poems from Other Cultures and Traditions

Contents

Introduction

This book accompanies the BBC School Television series, *Roots and Water*. It makes use of interviews conducted in preparation for the series, and refers to the film versions of the various poems around which the series is built. Both the book and programmes take as their subject matter the ten 'Poems from Other Cultures and Traditions' chosen for the NEAB GCSE anthology, examining from the year 2000 until 2002. This material is also suitable for study in other contexts, including the coursework element of other GCSE syllabuses.

'Other Cultures and Traditions' is a curious notion. The phrase appears in the Programmes of Study for Reading in the National Curriculum, where it serves as an acknowledgement that there is more to literature in English than 'the English literary heritage'. Both terms point to the awkwardness of categorising poems in terms of their authors' country of origin. The poems in this selection are written by poets born in a variety of places, some of whom have chosen to live in England, and all of whom have chosen to write in the English language. In their recorded interviews, these writers consider directly the notion of cultural identity, and their own sense of belonging, or not belonging, to particular cultures and traditions.

There is a great deal of poetry in the NEAB's GCSE syllabus. Each teacher will wish to select from among the ten poems and use them as a focus for developing as wide a range of skills as possible. This book is designed to support that kind of approach. It contains a variety of non-fiction texts, both in the form of interviews and other biographical material, and in the form of illustrative texts which can be used to enlarge understanding of the ideas and experiences which the poems present. It also contains a small selection of additional poems by each writer, chosen for their accessibility and relevance to the poem under discussion.

The film versions of the key texts in the programmes offer distinctive ways of reading the poems, responding creatively to textual details, and developing interpretations which may challenge, as well as illuminate, the reader's own. These films can also be used as media texts – examples of that broad genre of narrative shorts of which music videos and television advertisements are also often a part. The book contains examples of film treatments used in the making of the programme and suggestions for appropriate media coursework assignments.

Finally, the subject matter of the poems, all of which deal in some way with cultural values and cultural identity, can contribute powerfully to the personal and social education of the student. Several of the authors speak in their poems and in their interviews about forging a personal identity in a context of cultural tension or complexity and about the human values to which each is ultimately committed.

The pages headed 'Exploring the Text' try to take account of this range of possibilities, and the questions are therefore open in nature, rather than directed at specific points of interpretation. The notes refer only to those things which cannot easily be found in a dictionary.

Nick Jones

Thinking about poetry

One of the characteristic things about poetry is its richness or density of meaning. Poets work closely on language – they make it do as much as possible in the space of a small number of words. That's why poems need reading more slowly, and more often, than other kinds of text.

This quality of concentration is characteristic of all poetry whatever cultural tradition it comes from. It reflects the nature of poetry as an expressive art – that what a poem says or does matters to the person who is writing it. It's what enables poems to lodge memorably in our minds, and to go on extending and deepening their meanings over time.

Studying poetry in school is at least partly about learning to appreciate what goes into a poem's making. This introductory section looks at four broad aspects of poetic craft which contribute, in different ways, to the meanings readers are able to make.

VOICE • register • tone

Poetry is written to be heard as well as seen. Poets listen to their drafts as they emerge and try to develop a distinctive voice or style across a body of work. One mark of enduring quality in a poet is a sense of a recognisable individual **voice**.

A poem's voice may also give us a sense of where it's coming from in a wider sense. It may be the characteristic voice of a particular place, time or literary tradition. The poets in this book are all living writers whose work has appeared within the last thirty years, and mainly within the last ten years. However, the variety of their biographies and the cultures in which they have worked have created marked distinctions of dialect and style.

Voice is not always a matter of simple identity. In some poems there is more than one voice – for example, when the poem is set out in the form of a dialogue. In some poems, the voice which has been adopted is that of a 'persona', a kind of character within the poem – so the 'I' of a poem is not always the author.

As with other kinds of writing, a poet's choice of **register** – of vocabulary and grammatical structures – will strongly affect the way a reader responds. Older poetry, in particular, is likely to sound 'more poetic' to contemporary ears. In the present century, following the example of modernism, absolutely any kind of language can be incorporated into poetry. Poets are great experimenters – there is pleasure in breaking rules, or playing with conventions, and also a power in using language adventurously or even shockingly, to find a way past the reader's more regular responses. There is a strong sense in which all poetry is a 'non-standard' form of the language.

The voice of a poem is often clearest when the poem is addressed directly to the reader, or to a third party whose conversation is overheard. This kind of voice will tend to be more personal, more like a drama than a written narrative. Twentieth-century poetry has modelled itself consistently on the cadences of speech, partly as a kind of democratising of poetic form. For some poets, the printed version of a poem is no more than an unsatisfactory transcript of a sequence of sounds. The emphasis on performance can, itself, affect the visual look of the work on the page.

The **tone** of a poem is best explained as the 'tone of voice' in which we imagine the poem to be spoken. From the tone, we get our sense of the poet's relationship to the reader – or the nature of the adopted persona. We may also pick up an expressed attitude towards the things described. The tone of a writer's work is sometimes so consistent that it becomes a part of what we recognise about her or him. In other cases, tone may vary both between poems and within a single poem, as the variations of voice and mood track the development of the poem's ideas.

Questions to ask yourself when thinking about VOICE

- How would I read this poem aloud? Is there anything in the voice of the poem which makes it difficult for me to read it aloud?

- Does the voice in this poem sound as if it's coming from a particular time or place?

- Who seems to be speaking in this poem? Who is the poem speaking to?

- Does the poem's tone of voice suggest a particular attitude towards, or relationship with, the reader?

- Is the poem characterised by a particular kind of vocabulary or sentence?

- Does the tone of voice suggest a particular attitude towards the subject matter of the poem?

- Is there more than one kind of voice in the poem? If so, what's the relationship between the two?

FORM • pattern • typography

Poetic **form** is to do with a poem's shape and pattern, both on the page and to the ear. One basic distinction is between metrical and non-metrical forms. Metrical poetry (or verse) is composed to fit a recurring pattern of rhythmical stresses, and often a rhyme scheme as well. The poem is laid out in regular blocks. The verse unit ranges from simple couplets to elaborate stanzas. Most song lyrics are metrical, to match the repeating patterns of musical composition. In poems of this kind, the meaning is, to some extent, made to fit the shape: the poet's choice of words and word order must take account of the rhyme scheme and the pattern of syllables.

In a non-metrical poem, on the other hand, the structure is 'organic' in the sense that it finds its own shape line by line, resulting in irregular patterns and variable paragraphs, rather than fixed stanzas. This form of poetry, sometimes called 'free verse', is built around the varying rhythms of the speaking voice, and of natural grammar, so is likely to sound more like a person talking.

Before 1900, virtually all English poetry was metrical. During the twentieth century, the Modern movement greatly extended the boundaries of what was considered poetic, so that any kind of language could be incorporated into a poem, and irregular forms became much more common. Yet traditional metre hasn't died out and many contemporary poets are still strongly attracted to its music and its feeling of durability.

Although some modern poetry (like some modern art or music) may appear entirely fragmentary and 'unstructured', most poets consider carefully how a poem sounds and appears. In a non-metrical poem, poetic **patterning** can be achieved in other ways, particularly through the repetition of words and phrases to build rhythmic and rhetorical energy. Poets will often seek a balance or tension between regular and irregular elements, as in 'syllabic' verse (of which the haiku form is an example) where the rhythm is variable, but the length of each line is arithmetically fixed. The majority of the poems in this book – all by living writers – take a non-metrical form, but build pattern and cohesion in other ways, through consistency of voice or line length, repeated grammatical structures or the echoes of half-rhymes or rhythmic fragments.

Another aspect of form is to do with the visual presentation of the poem on the page, or its **typography**. Traditionally, each line of a metrical poem is marked with a capital letter (regardless of sentence grammar), and indentations at the start of lines correspond to rhyme patterns. There is also a tendency for punctuation to coincide with the ends of lines and for each stanza to end with a full stop so that 'running on' the grammatical sense across a line break is a definite variation on the established pattern.

In non-metrical poetry, lines are likely to be more fluid, varying in length for specific effects and running on as a matter of course. Capitals are used as in prose, to begin sentences, rather than lines. Lines aren't marked so emphatically, and punctuation marks, which are a written convention, may be replaced by spaces representing the breath-pauses of speech. In a lot of modern poetry, the upper case and other punctuation marks have been eliminated altogether. Instead, the poet relies on line breaks and spacing to suggest how the poem should be voiced and understood. Different fonts (typefaces) and other variations can also be used to structure or emphasise.

Questions to ask yourself when thinking about FORM

- Is there a formal structure to this poem? Does it have a regular metrical pattern? Is there a rhyme scheme? Could someone sing this poem?

- Are there other ways in which this poem is patterned? What elements of repetition are there?

- Is this structure associated with a particular type of poem or particular period?

- What typographic conventions does the poem use, or not use? How does that contribute to the style or voice of the poem?

- Do any of these things help me to understand what kind of poem this is?

- Does the form of the poem emphasise any aspect of its mood or meaning?

IMAGERY • representation • metaphor

In poetry, an '**image**' is a sharply-focused descriptive detail. This is most often a visual detail (like an image in a film), though it can evoke any of the senses. It is through their images that poets engage the reader's imagination, evoking a place, mood or person, and also influencing us to respond in particular ways.

At the core of any image is a noun. Adjectives may extend and adjust the noun's meaning, as may the verbs which go with it, but the noun is what we see – so it will be a concrete (i.e. non-abstract) noun. Images work because 'things' carry meanings of various kinds, depending on the context in which they occur – they can imply an event, an emotion or a wider idea.

Images will often mean different things to different people, depending on their experience both as readers and as human beings, and one of the things poets do is to train us to see things in a different way. However, images also work through the shared meanings and associations which any culture develops around particular words or objects – their connotations. When an image is consistently recognised and interpreted in the same way, it becomes an established symbol within that culture.

Images can be either literal or figurative. In the case of literal imagery, connotation is achieved through selecting and emphasising details. A helpful connection here is between the concept of 'imagery' familiar to poetry lessons and the concept of '**representation**' in media studies.

When an image is figurative (or metaphorical – the words are interchangeable), its connotations are doubly emphasised since that is the point of the shift into figurative language: the thing described acquires the connotations of the thing named. For that reason, **metaphors** tend to feature strongly in what is sometimes termed 'emotive language', whether in poetry or in propaganda. Metaphors are also a means of converting abstract ideas into the physical images with which poetry deals.

Discussion of metaphor in the classroom is sometimes sidetracked into the essentially trivial distinction between 'simile' and 'metaphor' as alternative forms of 'linguistic device'. What matters is not the difference between the two, but the way both are used to superimpose meanings.

A metaphor is not so much a decorative 'device' as a way of thinking. Some metaphors are so deep-rooted that they structure the way almost everybody thinks – that life is a journey, that love is a fire, that argument is a kind of warfare. Others, in poetry especially, are acts of invention, in which one object is fused imaginatively with another, in order to startle or disturb the reader into some fresh perception. Careful attention to the images in a poem helps to put us directly in touch with the poet's imaginative vision, and with the values and attitudes which underlie it.

Questions to ask yourself when thinking about IMAGERY

- Which image first caught my attention? Which image is most central to what the poem has to say? Did any of the images surprise me?

- Are some of these images metaphorical? What things are being superimposed here? How does this add to my understanding?

- Do some of the images suggest strong positive or negative connotations?

- Do certain images connect with each other, to create a particular mood, attitude or impression?

- Are there contrasting images in the poem? How do these contribute to meaning? Do they relate to shifts in the narrative or argument?

NARRATIVE • argument • viewpoint

The **narrative** of a text is the order in which events, images or ideas are recorded, and the way in which they relate to each other. In looking at the narrative sequence of a poem, we are focusing on the way it has been constructed in terms of the development of its content.

Many poems are like miniature stories. They record a series of events, perhaps leading to some kind of insight at the end. First person narratives give the appearance of personal memories. Third person narratives or descriptions can seem more detached, with less of a sense that the poet is present in the text.

The past is the natural tense for narratives, though telling a story in the present tense can produce a sense of reliving the experience, moment by moment. Looking carefully at the tenses used in a poem will help to establish its chronology, and to distinguish, for example, 'how it used to be' (also signalled by words like 'once' or 'then') from how it is now, or how it might be in the future.

The distinction between narrative and argument isn't a hard and fast one – narratives can be used to illustrate arguments, for example. But many poems are built around the logical development of ideas, rather than the recounting of events. **Arguments** proceed by asking questions, stating propositions, referring to examples, drawing conclusions. However, while other kinds of writers deal in abstract debate, poets are more likely to make their point through resonant images, or other less direct means. This way of organising a poem is particularly common to those written in the second person.

The underlying structure of a poem can usually be detected through its use of connectives. In the case of argument, these are likely to be logical conjunctions such as 'if', 'so', 'because', 'but', 'yet', rather than the conjunctions of time used in narratives.

Another way of thinking about the development of a poem is in terms of its transitions – the term used in film editing for the way shots are joined. Spaces between sections in a poem may signal a break in continuity: a kind of fade out and in. One image may effectively dissolve into another, or the cut may be more abrupt. And as with films, poems often leave it to the reader to make sense of such transitions for themselves.

Thinking about the sequence of a narrative or an argument in this way may draw attention to the **viewpoint** of the poem and take us back to the sense of 'voice' with which we started. We need to work out whose voice we are hearing, and who is seeing whatever is being described. Is the viewpoint fixed or does it shift between different observers, or over time? As with any other text, the beginning and the ending of a poem are likely to carry a particular kind of force.

Questions to ask yourself when looking at NARRATIVE

- Is the poem divided into sections? Do these correspond to shifts in the development of the story or the argument? How does the poet manage the transitions between them?

- What tenses are used here? Is there a dominant tense, or a mixture? What does this tell me about the poem?

- Which pronouns are used? Is this text broadly first, second or third person? Or is it a mixture?

- From what viewpoint is the story told? Where would the camera be if the poem were filmed? Does the viewpoint change?

- Is it clear what kind of sequence this is – narration, argument, description?

- Which are the key connectives? What do they tell me about the way the poem develops?

- What questions does the poet ask? What questions are left for the reader to ask?

Thinking about culture

The National Curriculum for English requires all pupils to study texts 'from other cultures and traditions'. This section looks briefly at the meanings of those words and of some of the other words that come to mind when we start to think about culture, tradition or 'otherness'.

The ten poets featured in this selection belong to a variety of nations and ethnic groups; they have also written poems which, in various ways, invite us to think about culture and identity. So these two pages point to themes which will recur throughout this anthology, a kind of introductory thesaurus.

CULTURE • tradition • heritage

A **culture** is a way of life, and a way of thinking about the world, which is characteristic of a particular group. In its oldest sense, the word is related to 'agriculture', and means anything which grows and is tended over time. Later, by a kind of metaphor, it comes to imply 'cultivation' in a different sense – an educated refinement of manners and artistic taste. In this sense, the word becomes laden with particular values and preferences – associated with 'high culture', for example, rather than 'low' or popular culture. But in modern usage, 'culture' refers to the whole complex of thought and behaviour characteristic of a people – everything from their basic religious beliefs and values through to changing preferences of fashion or lifestyle. A further complication is that in many cultures we can distinguish between a dominant mainstream and various kinds of subcultural groups, including those who are pushing to develop the culture in new ways, and those who still cling to how it used to be in the past.

Traditions are those parts of a culture which have been handed on from the past, and maintained into the present, and include both the things people do and the things they remember or believe to be true. Traditional practices often survive most strongly in the context of craft skills and in the ceremonies surrounding religious belief, even where their earlier religious significance has faded. Traditions also take the form of stories and legends which are passed on orally through generations. Traditions are not always fixed: to study a 'literary tradition', for example, is to trace forms and styles which

evolve over generations, as one writer learns from another. Traditions can be a source of stability and strength in a culture, but they can also be a brake on development, so to call someone 'a traditionalist' may imply they are too attached to old ways, especially in contexts that call for a different way of thinking.

The word **heritage** also refers to something handed on from the past. Its origin is from the word 'inheritance', but here the emphasis tends to be on objects or places of value rather than ways of doing things. 'Our cultural heritage' includes lists of buildings or landscapes which should be preserved, classic works of art and anything valued for its age and rarity. In the National Curriculum, the phrase 'the English literary heritage' is used to refer to a list of authors officially considered to represent the best of English writing, particularly writing before the year 1900. The 'heritage industry', which has grown rapidly in recent years, makes money out of people's interest in the past (or from reconstructions of the past as people like to imagine it).

IDENTITY • roots • beliefs

Most of the poetry in this book is concerned in some way with the question of **identity**. Identity is a complex notion because people define themselves both in terms of the groups to which they belong, and also sometimes in opposition to those groups. Another complication is that people belong simultaneously to a number of different kinds of group: by birth to an ethnic community; by passport to a nation; by faith and upbringing to a religion, or to no religion; by wealth and education to a particular social class and by various kinds of preference to a whole range of other possible categories.

Language is one of the strongest of these sources of identification. The mother tongue links children to the world of their parents and carries its own set of values and ways of seeing things. Local dialects foster a sense of local belonging, just as as the adoption of unfamiliar forms of slang, jargon or accent (or a new language altogether) can mark someone's transfer to a different subcultural group.

The term '**roots**' is widely used to refer to the way personal identity can be rooted in, and nurtured by, an awareness or rediscovery of historical origins. It's a powerful metaphor, linking the natural history of blood ties and 'the family tree' to a sense of origin in the soil of a particular homeland. Sometimes that land is a nation, a motherland; sometimes it is simply a certain kind of landscape. To be rooted in this sense is to know family loyalty, to take pride in ethnicity, to honour ancestors. The commitment to roots may be particularly powerful in those cases where these connections have been, in some way, attacked or suppressed.

In addition, at the core of each person's identity are their **beliefs**, both what they believe to be the case, and what they 'believe in' in a different sense – the values they personally hold to be important. To call something a 'belief' implies that there are others who see things differently. When someone's personal values come into conflict with those of the cultural group to which they otherwise belong, they find themselves in a situation of dissent, and dissent can easily be perceived as betrayal. A 'radical' is, literally, someone who attacks the roots.

MIGRATION • otherness • diversity

The cultural complexity of the modern world has resulted from a number of historical processes. One is the redrawing of political boundaries through conquest or colonisation so that even when staying where they are, people find themselves a part of somewhere else. A second process, which has often followed the first, is that of **migration**, either from economic need or to escape political persecution. 'Emigration' refers to this experience from the perspective of the person who is leaving, usually in the hope of finding something better in a new world. 'Immigration' is the same process seen from the perspective of the receiving nation. Following disasters or atrocities, huge numbers of people may become involuntary migrants or refugees. Historically, the most far-reaching example of uprooting has been the enforced migration of the slave trade, which over the course of two centuries resulted in the transfer of several million people from Africa to the Americas.

Both the moving of boundaries, and the moving of peoples, results in the creation of minorities whose roots are somewhere other than where they live. The immediate experience of refugees or economic migrants is of displacement and dispossession, often with a wrenching sense of loss and exile. Over time, the choice for each generation is to find a balance between assimilation into the majority culture, ultimately through intermarriage, and nurturing the roots of the old 'home' culture, maintaining separate enclaves, and so continuing to be perceived as 'other' by the host community.

In the context of the national English curriculum, the word 'other' is used specifically to identify works of literature 'other than the English literary heritage'. It implies a positive broadening of the reader's horizons and a recognition of English as an international language. But in the wider context, the word 'other' can also be used to imply 'alien' with all its connotations of isolation, hostility and rejection. (People can, of course, feel 'alienated' by aspects of their own culture.)

This is the sense of **otherness** that leads to intolerance – where the notion of a person's 'identity' is based on negative perceptions of what people are not. The spirit of nationalism, for example, is often characterised by antagonism to people of neighbouring states. Racism is the rejection and persecution of others, based chiefly on differences of skin colour. Adopted as state policy, it takes forms of systematic injustice: apartheid (in South Africa) and segregation (in the USA and elsewhere) are prominent twentieth-century examples. A third 'ism' of this kind is sectarianism, in which differences of religious faith lead to fanatical hatred both within and between religions, and to the often murderous overriding of human rights.

History has shown, and continues to show, that what begins as private prejudice and hostility can grow into large scale oppression and persecution. In the multiracial and multicultural communities which characterise so much of the contemporary world, 'otherness' need not mean hostility and struggle. A commitment to **diversity**, based on equality of respect, is not just the toleration of differences, but their celebration as a source of personal and cultural enrichment.

Thinking about film

The *Roots and Water* television programmes contain filmed versions of all ten of the poems in the NEAB's GCSE anthology. In many ways, interpreting a poem on film is similar to interpreting a poem in your head. You have to find sounds and images to match those suggested by the text. However, as film-making is a technically complex process, it calls for a series of largely collaborative decisions, made in relation to a range of creative and technical choices.

The process is built around three kinds of script.
• The first stage is the writing of a film 'treatment': a kind of first draft or outline proposal, set out, shot-by-shot, alongside the text of the poem, showing how the filmed images and the soundtrack will interpret the poet's words. (Some examples of treatments are included in this book.)
• Once agreed, the treatment is converted into a more detailed shooting script. During shooting, those original ideas are likely to develop further in response to actual locations, performers and so on. The raw camera footage produced by director and crew is then time-coded for editing.
• The third (post-production) stage involves the creation of an 'edit decision list', based on a careful viewing and discussion of the images recorded. This leads to a rough cut, selecting and ordering the images to be used in the film, and then to the final cut, including detailed transitions, the full soundtrack and any special post-production effects.

Making a film of a poem means creating a work in one medium which is a response to a work in another – like a song setting or a book illustration. The film is only one interpretation of the poem, mainly the director's, though it is influenced by other members of the production team. Thinking specifically about the technical choices made during film-making is a way of gaining insight both into the films themselves and the poems behind them.

CAMERA IMAGE • frame • viewpoint

The selection of images to appear in the film will have been decided, in broad terms, at the treatment stage. A film is unlikely to offer visual equivalents of everything mentioned in a poem. Some of the film images may have no direct reference to images 'in' the text, but nonetheless be suggested by it. Interpretation is a matter of selection and emphasis and also of bringing things to the poem. During shooting, the important choices are to do with the composition of the shots.

Shots are **framed** in terms of subject and background, and this relates to the angle and distance from which a shot is taken. In a general way, the 'setting' of a film corresponds to the idea of setting in a literary text. Long shots, which include plenty of background, are conventionally used for 'establishing shots' – the equivalent of describing the scene. Where the background is visible, does it relate directly to the narrative or suggest things about a character or a style of life? In close-ups, the background becomes less visible, and the attention may be focused instead on what is going on inside the character's mind, particularly if the close-up is full face.

There is also a choice between a static and a moving frame. Should the camera remain fixed while the action moves? Or should the camera follow the action in some way by tracking (camera moves around subject), panning (camera swivels to follow the subject) or zooming (altering the apparent distance from the subject)?

These decisions are important in that they contribute to a sense of **viewpoint**. In general, the camera operates impersonally ('in the third person', we could say) without any suggestion of who is doing the watching. The viewer sees what the camera sees. At other times, the camera may be signalling a particular viewpoint. Alternating close-ups draw the viewer into a dialogue while 'reaction shots' of an actor's face encourage us to imagine their feelings. Camera angles that draw attention to themselves (by being unusually high or low, or by framing an aperture) sometimes imply an observer in a particular position. Sudden movements, or a prowling camera, involve the viewer more consciously in the act of viewing. 'Pulling' the focus during the course of a shot, say from foreground to background, mimics the act of noticing something.

Questions to ask yourself when thinking about the CHOICE AND COMPOSITION OF IMAGES

- Which images from the poem will be recreated in the film?
- What images will be added to it?
- Which shots will establish the scene?
- Which shots will be in close-up?
- At which points will the camera move?
- Will any of the shots be taken from an unusual angle? What will be the effect of that?

TONE • lighting • effects

There are also choices to be made at the shooting stage about light and colour – things which strongly affect the tone of a visual image. A director may compose a shot in terms of the range of colours on the screen (rather in the way an artist may choose a limited palette) so as to create a certain mood or ambience.

'Natural' light (which tends to mean, in practice, light which is artificial but unobtrusive) creates a sense of mood by suggesting a particular time, season, or weather. 'Expressive' lighting, on the other hand, is a more direct way of suggesting a particular mood or tone. Over-exposure or bleaching, for example, can create a subjective feel, suggestive perhaps of distant memories. A whole style of thriller – 'film noir' – was developed in the 1940s around the use of darkness, back-lighting and dramatic contrasts of light and shadow.

Soft or diffused lighting, often in association with 'soft-focus' and the use of dissolves, creates a dreamier, more lyrical style. Particularly in the case of short films, these effects can be sustained so as to give a 'look' to the cinematography which becomes part of the way the film interprets its subject.

The choices made during shooting can be supplemented or even altered during the post-production stage through the use of technical effects. Digital editing, in particular, opens up a range of non-naturalistic effects. Post-production techniques can be used to slow down or speed up the action, to alter the range of colours in a shot or to use 'paint' effects to stylise the image. Similarly, the range of images may be extended at this stage by using archive footage or stills.

Questions to ask yourself when thinking about LIGHTING AND TONE

- What will the dominant style of lighting be ?
- Will there be variations between images?
- What mood or tone will this create?
- Will any special effects be used to stylise the images?

EDITING • transitions • narrative

The main decisions to be taken at the post-production stage relate to the **editing** of the film, to the order and manner in which the shots are fitted together. Editing conventions are therefore equivalent to the grammar or syntax of a written text.

As with lighting or camera angles, the choice is between a style of editing that draws attention to itself and one that doesn't. 'Continuity editing' achieves an effect of seamlessness or invisibility and encourages the viewers to accept what is happening on the screen as a form of reality. This set of conventions is based on matched cuts, synchronising of sound and image, and naturalised rules for angles and sequencing. Most conventional television drama, for example, works in just this way. The alternative is to draw deliberate attention to the passage from one image to the next – a kind of disruption of the visual syntax. MTV (music television) is the most obvious example of this style of editing in which the sequence of images is sometimes held together only by the soundtrack.

There are broadly four types of **transition** between images.

1   The simple *cut*, used for continuity in the way described above, or alternatively to 'jump' from one image to the next.

2   The *fade* to (or from) black – conventionally, a means of signalling the end (or the beginning) of a sequence.

3   The *wipe*, in which one image is displaced by another moving across it: digital editing allows for a range of such effects.

4   The *dissolve*, where two images, one fading in and one fading out, are briefly superimposed on each other.

Each of these choices can be used to create a particular effect: digital wipes, for example, are attention-grabbing and so feature widely in certain kinds of television advertising, while dissolves are more lyrical and suggestive of the passing of time.

In a similar way, we might say, modern poets experiment in their own way with the 'jump-cuts' and 'dissolves' of syntax, using space on the page to organise meaning, juxtaposing images unexpectedly, cross-fading between memories.

The pace of a film depends almost entirely on the editing – the number of shots/transitions per minute is a good indication of this, as well as the balance of cuts and dissolves. Editing is also the way in which the film-maker tells a story. The main transitions operate like paragraph markers, establishing a new location, involving us in the perceptions and reactions of the characters, signalling a flashback or a move forward through time. All the features of **narrative** discussed above in relation to poetry thus have their equivalent in the sequencing of the film.

Questions to ask yourself when thinking about the EDITING of a film

- Which will be the main points of transition?
- What different types of transition will be used?
- Will the style of editing draw attention to itself?
- What sort of pace will the film have?
- What will be the effect of these decisions?

SOUNDTRACK

We tend to think of film as a visual medium, but shouldn't underestimate the contribution made by a film's audio track. Cameras also record sound, and the natural sound accompanying the filmed action may be retained in the final edit. The final soundtrack is likely to be created after the event, at the post-production stage, and may include elements which are not directly related to what is visible on the screen.

In the case of poem-films, the soundtrack is likely to contain the words of the poem. A performance of the text, whether by the poet or by another reader, is itself an interpretation of the poem's meaning. A reading to camera gives a physical identity to the voice of the poem; voice-overs tend to reach more directly into the listener's ear, and also open up a greater range of visual possibilities.

As well as the words of the poem, the soundtrack will often include music or other sound, designed to supplement or interpret what is seen on the screen. Film scores are a powerful source of mood, atmosphere and emotion, even when the viewer is so gripped by the images that they barely notice the music they are hearing. Absolute silence in film is rare so can be a particularly effective 'sound effect'.

Questions to ask yourself when thinking about the SOUNDTRACK of a film

- Will the poem be read as a voice-over? What style of reading will this be?
- Will the soundtrack include sounds recorded during filming, such as dialogue?
- Will there be music at any point, and what kind of music will it be?
- Will there be other kinds of sound effects?

With knife and gimlet care he worked away at this on Sundays,
explored its knotted hurts, cutting his way
along its yellow whorls until his hands could feel
how it had swelled and shivered, breathing air,
its weathered green burning to rings of time,
its contoured grain still tuned to roots and water.

Kamau Brathwaite, *Ogun*

ROOTS & WATER

Culture is what the poet comes from and returns to over & over & over again & in the end. It is his home, it is his drum, it is his dream: the shared collective conscious experience of a people, with submerged underdrones – ghosts, spirits, sky-juices, ancestors, immemorial memories...

Kamau Brathwaite, *Barabajan Poems*

Any society is a society in conflict, and any anthology
of a society's poetry that does not reflect this, is a lie.

Tom Leonard, *Literature, Dialogue, Democracy*

I was born a foreigner.
I carried on from there
to become a foreigner everywhere.

Imtiaz Dharker, *Minority*

I have crossed an ocean
I have lost my tongue
from the root of the old one
a new one has sprung

Grace Nichols, *i is a long-memoried woman*

Sujata **Bhatt**

Sujata Bhatt was born in 1956 in Ahmedabad, India, where her mother tongue was Gujarati. When she was still an infant, her family moved to Pune (or Poona), near Bombay, where the official language is Marathi. Sujata then spent three years in New Orleans, USA, where she first learned English. On returning to Pune, aged eight, she attended an English-speaking school. In 1968, her family moved permanently to America, where she attended high school and university. While studying Creative Writing at the University of Iowa, she met her German husband, with whom she moved to Bremen, in northern Germany, in 1987.

Her first book of poems, *Brunizem*, was published in England in 1988. (The word 'brunizem' is the name of a prairie soil found in Asia, Europe and North America.) Sujata Bhatt has also translated poems from Gujarati into English. *Search for my Tongue* is a long poem in three parts: the text printed in the anthology is an extract.

Sujata Bhatt introduces her work

It's strange for me to consider Bremen as home, but in a way it is. When I visit my parents or my brother, I think of myself when I was younger and I lived there, but I don't think I really consider that as home either. I have always thought of myself as an Indian who is outside India, and I would find it difficult to say I'm not Indian because for me that would mean disowning my parents. That's the deepest layer of my identity. Then I think identity can change according to where you live, and I think of myself as having attachments to several cultures, so in that sense, several identities. I don't think identity is something static. On a simple level, one's identity becomes different if one is a mother and things like that.

I think I'm fairly adaptable. In America there are many communities where Indians seem to be very segregated because they isolate themselves and have their own activities, which is fine, but I feel some of them don't interact with the society they're living in. I'm someone who likes to know where I am and I tend to be curious about other people...

I started writing poems and short stories when I was eight. I like to experiment and I like to try different ways of writing and different subjects. I see myself as an Indian poet who's been influenced by American and British

literature. I write mainly in English. A lot of Gujarati poetry is very traditional – the forms are strict, and it's a lot easier to rhyme in Gujarati. And in many of the north Indian languages, like Hindi and Bengali also, the literary language is very elevated. In twentieth-century British and American poetry, the language has become increasingly closer to the language of everyday speech.

I wrote *Search for my Tongue* long ago when I was twenty-two, so of course, in many ways it's a young person's poem and I think it explores feelings that I had that were very strong at that time. I wrote it when I was in Baltimore, in the USA, and at that time I was reading a lot of Gujarati and also English for university, and sometimes I would be thinking in two languages, and this poem grew out of that. And earlier, when I was about thirteen, and we had just been in America for a few months, I had written a poem in which I used a Gujarati word, and the teacher told me you can't use Gujarati in an English poem – only French or Spanish or Italian... And, of course, at that age, I just said 'Oh well' and I never tried it again. And then by the time I was twenty-two, I had read T S Eliot, and in his *Waste Land* he used Sanskrit words, so I felt, well, I could too. The poem was written very quickly. It was really a case where everything just flowed, and afterwards there was very little that I changed...

Lines 31-38 are a rough translation of lines 17-30. In English the word 'tongue' can mean 'language' and the tongue in your mouth, but in Gujarati it doesn't, so I have to use both words in the Gujarati – the word 'jeebh' is tongue, and then the word 'bhasha' is language. In Gujarati I have to say, 'like a fruit my language, my tongue, ripens in my mouth'. The stanza in English is slightly different...

From a recorded BBC telephone interview, Bremen, Germany, June 1998

Search for my Tongue

You ask me what I mean
by saying I have lost my tongue.
I ask you, what would you do
if you had two tongues in your mouth,
and lost the first one, the mother tongue,
and could not really know the other,
the foreign tongue.
You could not use them both together
even if you thought that way.
And if you lived in a place you had to
speak a foreign tongue,
your mother tongue would rot,
rot and die in your mouth
until you had to spit it out.
I thought I spit it out
but overnight while I dream,

મને હતું કે આખ્ખી જીભ આખ્ખી ભાષા,

(munay hutoo kay aakhee jeebh aakhee bhasha)

મેં થૂંકી નાખી છે.

(may thoonky nakhi chay)

પરં તુ રાત્રે સ્વપ્નામાં મારી ભાષા પાછી આવે છે.

(parantoo rattray svupnama man bhasha pachi aavay chay)

ફુલની જેમ મારી ભાષા મારી જીભ

(foolnee jaim man bhasha man jeebh)

મોઢામાં ખીલે છે.

(modhama kheelay chay)

ફૂલની જેમ મારી ભાષા મારી જીભ

(fullnee jaim man bhasha man jeebh)

મોઢામાં પાકે છે.

(modhama pakay chay)

it grows back, a stump of a shoot
grows longer, grows moist, grows strong veins,
it ties the other tongue in knots,
the bud opens, the bud opens in my mouth,
it pushes the other tongue aside.
Everytime I think I've forgotten,
I think I've lost the mother tongue,
it blossoms out of my mouth.

A Different History

Great Pan is not dead;
he simply emigrated
                to India.
Here, the gods roam freely,
disguised as snakes or monkeys;
every tree is sacred
and it is a sin
to be rude to a book.
It is a sin to shove a book aside
                    with your foot,
a sin to slam books down
                hard on a table,
a sin to toss one carelessly
                across a room.
You must learn how to turn the pages gently
without disturbing Sarasvati,
without offending the tree
from whose wood the paper was made.

2

Which language
has not been the oppressor's tongue?
Which language
truly meant to murder someone?
And how does it happen
that after the torture,
after the soul has been cropped
with a long scythe swooping out
of the conqueror's face –
the unborn grandchildren
grow to love that strange language.

NOTE
Search for my Tongue
The lines in Gujarati are translated in the lines
which then follow: see page 13.
A Different History
Great Pan: Greek nature god (cf. pantheism)
Sarasvati: Hindu goddess of knowledge

The Voices

First, a sound from an animal
you can never imagine.

Then: insect-rustle, fish-hush.

And then the voices became louder.

Voice of an angel who is newly dead.
Voice of a child who refuses
to ever become an angel with wings.

Voice of tamarinds.
Voice of the colour blue.
Voice of the colour green.
Voice of the worms.
Voice of the white roses.
Voice of the leaves torn by goats.
Voice of snake-spit.
Voice of the placenta.
Voice of the fetal heartbeat.
Voice of the scalped skull
whose hair hangs behind glass
in a museum.

I used to think there was
only one voice.
I used to wait
patiently for that one voice to return
to begin its dictation.

I was wrong.

I can never finish counting them now.
I can never finish
writing all they have to say.

Voice of the ghost who wants
to die again, but this time
in a brighter room with fragrant flowers
and different relatives.
Voice of the frozen lake.
Voice of the fog.
Voice of the air while it snows.
Voice of the girl
who still sees unicorns
and speaks to angels she knows by name.
Voice of pine tree sap.

And then the voices became louder.

Sometimes I hear them
laughing at my confusion.

And each voice insists
        and each voice knows
that it is the true one.

And each voice says: *follow me*
follow me and I will take you –

At the Flower Market

When we go to the flower market,
my daughter and I,
it's only to look around
not to buy.
For me it's to look at her
six-month-old face while she stares
at the colours and smells
the sour oozing of cut stems
the sweet soil of potted plants.
So many different leaves thrown together,
petals ruffled and fanning out so
even the least fragrant flowers *are* fragrant.
The lilies fighting giant sunflowers
for attention; rows of herbs arranged
beside tall *ficus benjamins*.

Today I stop by the expensive hibiscus
and bougainvillea, imprisoned
in plastic pots they sit like laboratory specimens
because this is Bremen.

In Poona
our bougainvillea bush
had grown to the size of an elephant.
The mauve bracts surrounding the flowers
would fly in the wind
like a thousand miniature paper kites.
And the hibiscus, so abundant,
those red trumpets with tongues
like golden worms curling out.

Still, I go by every stall in Bremen's
city centre flower market –
for no reason
except to watch my daughter's face open,
her confused curiosity
that makes me plan journeys.

NOTES
At the Flower Market
Bremen: German city where
the poet now lives
Poona: Indian city of the
poet's childhood

Search for my Tongue: exploring the text

(i) Practise reading the text of *Search for my Tongue* – the phonetic transcription (in brackets) enables non-Gujarati readers to produce an approximate version of the Gujarati script. Alternatively, listen to Sujata Bhatt's own reading on the audio tape.

- What common phrases can you think of involving the word 'tongue'?

  Which of these use 'tongue' in the sense of a physical body part, and which use 'tongue' in the abstract to mean 'language'?
  (If your group contains speakers of languages other than English, you may be able to include examples from that language as well.)

- How is the physicality of the tongue emphasised in the imagery of this poem?

- Read the information on page 13 about Sujata Bhatt, especially about her personal history as a language user. Does this information help you to deepen your understanding of *Search for my Tongue*?

- Lines 17-30 of *Search for my Tongue* are translated in the lines that then follow. So you could say that the poem would 'mean' the same if lines 17-30 were omitted. What would the poem have lost if they were?

- In Britain, there are over one hundred different minority languages in daily use. If you speak more than one language, try writing something – a poem, if you like – in both your languages, using *Search for my Tongue* as a model.

(ii) Watch the broadcast film version of *Search for my Tongue*.

- How do you think it was made?

- Is the film a faithful representation of the poem?

- Does it provoke ideas on language and the way we use it?

- What kind of film of this poem would you have made?

(iii) Read the additional poems by Sujata Bhatt on pages 14 and 15.

- *At the Flower Market* is another poem which can be read in relation to Sujata Bhatt's biography (page 13). Why do you think her daughter's reaction to the flowers makes her 'plan journeys'?

- Look up 'pantheism'. Does this help you to make sense of the first part of *A Different History*?

  What does the second part of that poem have to say about languages and military conquest?

  There's no direct connection between the two parts of *A Different History*. Can you think why the poet might have chosen to link them together under this title?

- How many of the voices in *The Voices* are imaginable as sounds? Do these voices have anything in common? What do you think the voices are offering the poet at the end of this poem?

Suggested writing tasks

1 *Search for my Tongue*

How does the form and the imagery of this poem convey the experience of speaking and thinking in two different languages?

2 *Search for my Tongue* and *Unrelated Incidents* by Tom Leonard

What have you learned from these poems about the connection between the language(s) people use, and their sense of personal identity?

3 *Search for my Tongue* and *Ogun* by Kamau Brathwaite

In both these poems, the poet writes about a search for something. What, in each case, does the search involve, and are there similarities in the two situations?

Tom **Leonard**

Tom Leonard introduces his work

I was born in 1944 in Glasgow, the fourth child of a Dublin man who worked as a railwayman in Scotland all his working life, and an Ayrshire woman who had given up her job in a dynamite factory when she married in 1933. My childhood upbringing was working class, west of Scotland, Irish Catholic.

When I left school, I worked as a government clerk in the employment service, then in a variety of jobs, including university bookshop assistant for a few years. While working in this shop, I studied at night and got enough exam passes to go to Glasgow University. I left after a couple of years without completing a degree, having among other things spent a lot of my time editing the university magazine. My first publication was *Six Glasgow Poems*, which I wrote while at university in 1967-8.

After getting married and working with the Post Office in London, I came back with my wife, Sonya, and our first child, to Glasgow, where we completed our degrees. My first writing fellowship was with Renfrew District Libraries. While there, I compiled from Paisley Central Library archives, the anthology *Radical Renfrew: Poetry from the French Revolution to the First World War*. This brought back into print sixty nineteenth-century poets from the west of Scotland, and was partly an exhumation of my own cultural roots as well as a guide for the public as to how to use the library service to establish their own roots.

I have tended to have my poetry published in a series of small-press booklets, these then being gathered together every now and again. My collection of twenty years' work, *Intimate Voices*, shared the Saltire Scottish Book of the Year Award in 1984. The title indicated that the work did not employ the bogus Public Voice that has been the curse of British poetry and culture since the nineteenth century.

My focus on 'the voice' in my work had two by-products over the years: an involvement in performance 'sound poetry' (my own work being composed for stereo tapes, placards and voice) and an increasingly explicit awareness of the political nature of voice in British culture. The sequence *nora's place*, collected in *Reports from the Present* is, I think, as far as I have been able, so far, to make a poetry using my own ordinary, working-class, west of Scotland speech in the named 'banality' of daily living, that is still poetry. Ideally, I would like my work to constitute a republic of voices, grounded on a consistent personality and philosophy of language.

This is an edited version of a reference biography requested in the USA.

Poetry

the pee as in pulchritude,
oh pronounced ough
as in bough

the ee rather poised
(pronounced ih as in wit)
then a languid high tea…

pause: then the coda –
ray pronounced rih
with the left eyebrow raised
– what a gracious bouquet!

Poetry.
Poughit. rih.

That was my education
– and nothing to do with me.

from **Situations Theoretical and Contemporary**

And their judges spoke with one dialect,
but the condemned spoke with many voices.

And the prisons were full of many voices,
but never the dialect of the judges.

And the judges said:
　　　　　　'No-one is above the law.'

from Unrelated Incidents

(2)

ifyi stull
huvny
wurkt oot
thi diff-
rince tween
yir eyes
n
yir ears;
– geez peace,
pal!

fyi stull
huvny
thoata lang-
wij izza
sound-system;
fyi huvny
hudda thingk
aboot thi dif-
frince tween
sound
n object n
symbol; well,
ma innocent
wee
friend – iz
god said ti
adam:

a doant kerr
fyi caw it
an apple
ur
an aippl-
jist leeit
alane!

from Unrelated Incidents

(3)

this is thi
six a clock
news thi
man said n
thi reason
a talk wia
BBC accent
iz coz yi
widny wahnt
mi ti talk
aboot thi
trooth wia
voice lik
wanna yoo
scruff. if
a toktaboot
thi trooth
lik wanna yoo
scruff yi
widny thingk
it wuz troo.
jist wanna yoo
scruff tokn.
thirza right
way ti spell
ana right way
ti tok it. this
is me tokn yir
right way a
spellin. this
is ma trooth.
yooz doant no
thi trooth
yirsellz cawz
yi canny talk
right. this is
the six a clock
nyooz. belt up.

A Summer's Day

yir eyes ur
eh
a mean yir

pirrit this wey
ah a thingk yir
byewtifl like ehm

fact
fact a thingk yir
ach a luvyi thahts

thahts
jist thi wey it iz like
thahts ehm
aw ther iz ti say

Fathers and Sons

I remember being ashamed of my father
when he whispered the words out loud
reading the newspaper.

"Don't you find
the use of phonetic urban dialect
rather constrictive?"
asks a member of the audience.

The poetry reading is over.
I will go home to my children.

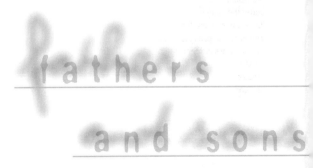

A Handy Form for Artists
to use in connection with the City of Culture

Date as postmark

Dear

Thank you for your *invitation*/*commission** for me to *participate*/*contribute*/*display*/*write an article*/*write a play*/*write a poem*/*sing*/*discuss*/*act*/*conduct*/*read from my work** / play the   *†,

at   Glasgow on   the   of   1990.

I note that this   *is being wholly or partly sponsored from funds allocated for*/*uses advertising material that mentions*/*is being described as part of*/*does not effectively dissociate itself from*/*
†
the so-called 'City of Culture' programme of events.

I regret that I cannot accept your *invitation*/*commission*/ because

it is a matter of conscience too tedious to explain/City Culture *yes* City of a Culture *yes* City of Culture *no*/ *the slogan is a nasty piece of advertising language meaning: a) places and people are worth something as to whether or not they can be described as 'of Culture' b) that desirable thing-to-be-owned, Culture, is now owned by Glasgow c) City of Culture = Person of Culture = Someone who does not enter the drawing room with cheese on their whiskers*/ *it is as much an insult to Beethoven and Rembrandt as it is to so-called 'community art' and to any citizen past or present*/ *any participating artist, work of art, or event will appear within the programme as an exemplification of this right-wing tourist slogan*/*critical of 'left-wing' works within the programme will function as the 'antibodies necessary to keep the body politic healthy' - which it most certainly isn't*/ *come-on-in the labour's cheap and the entertainment's good*/*come-on-in Razor King has been burried with his bunnit*/*†

and because I am fed up with

the relentless use of the word 'celebration' in connection with Glasgow by mediapersons/ *my children getting crap food at school because of dinnerschool cutbacks*/ *with public service workers being laid off, or their wages driven down 'so that we can hold on to the tender'*/ *with my health service being destroyed what about people with things like emphysema, it's not all smoking this city is cold and damp*/*with it being a crime to be under 25*/ *with them agreeing to sell the council houses*/ *with the unemployment figures, and all the other statistics, everybody knows they're shite, when am I going to turn on my radio or television and hear honest language*/ *with the land around Glasgow practically crackling with radioactivity you soon won't even be able to go to Saltcoats for a paddle*/ *why do the lamb chops in the butchers glow in the dark*/ *why don't they put turnstiles on the housing schemes and make them Deprived Heritage Museums*/ *with all this Mr Even Happier nonsense*/*
†

Yours sincerely

(Citizen of Glasgow)*

* delete if inapplicable   † insert other if necessary

NOTES
In 1990, Glasgow ran a 'City of Culture' promotion, involving an extensive programme of arts events. Tom Leonard produced this 'Handy Form' in an attempt to avoid having anything to do with it. It appears in *Reports from the Present: Selected Works 1982-94*.

Mr Even Happier: a reference to another promotional campaign under the slogan 'Glasgow's Miles Better'. *The Razor King*: a reference to Glasgow's old reputation for street violence, which these campaigns were designed to displace.

Unrelated Incidents 3: exploring the text

(i) There are seven *Unrelated Incidents* in all, each a reflection on some aspect of language and politics. In No.3, the speaker puts into his own words the political attitude (as it seems to him) of the BBC newsreader. (You need to read the poem aloud to appreciate its precise phonetic transcription of the Glaswegian voice. It works rather like the phonetic version of Gujarati script in Sujata Bhatt's poem, *Search for my Tongue*.)

- What would be lost if you 'translated' this poem into standard English?

- 'What I hate about the news,' Tom Leonard has written, 'is its definite article.' Can you see what he means by this? (The word 'the' is known grammatically as 'the definite article'.)

(ii) The passage on page 21 is taken from the introduction to a book on *The Dialects of England* by Peter Trudgill. What did you learn from reading this page? What would you say is Trudgill's general attitude towards variety in language? Do you make any connections here with Tom Leonard's ideas?

(iii) Tom Leonard produced his satirical *Handy Form* (page 19) in reaction to the 1990 promotion of Glasgow as City of Culture, 1990. Can you work out from the form what Tom Leonard's objection was to the phrase 'City of Culture'? Why would he not object to 'City Culture' or 'City of a Culture'? (It might be helpful to see what it says about the word 'culture' on page 7.)

(iv) For understandable reasons, Tom Leonard had reservations about the BBC making a film version of this poem. What do you visualise when you read the poem? Can you imagine a film version which underlined, rather than undermined, the point Tom Leonard is making in this poem?

(v) Read the other poems by Tom Leonard on pages 17 and 18.

- The title of *A Summer's Day* recalls the opening of one of Shakespeare's most quoted sonnets, 'Shall I compare thee to a summer's day' (No.18). What is this title up to?

- Which of the dialects mentioned in Trudgill's article (page 21) is 'the dialect of the judges' mentioned in *Situations Theoretical and Contemporary*, do you think?

- The six Tom Leonard poems included here all deal in some way with what the poet says is one of his main concerns – 'the political nature of voice in British culture' (see page 17). What do these poems, taken together, have to say on this subject? (We call something 'political' if it has to do with power and authority, and who holds it.)

Suggested writing tasks

1 *Unrelated Incidents 3*

What does this poem have to say about the relationship between language and power?

2 *Unrelated Incidents* and *Search for my Tongue* by Sujata Bhatt

What have you learned from these poems about the connection between the language(s) people use, and their sense of personal identity?

3 *Unrelated Incidents* and *Half-caste* by John Agard

Readers have found both humour and anger in these poems. Write about your own response to the two poems in those terms.

4 *Unrelated Incidents* and *Nothing's Changed* by Tatamkhulu Afrika

In different ways, both these poems can be seen as 'post-colonial' poems. What evidence do the two poets find of continuing domination, and how do they respond to it?

Language variety in England

One thing that is important to many English people is where they are from. The country is full of football supporters whose main concern is for the club of their childhood, even though they may now live hundreds of miles away. Local newspapers criss-cross the country on their way to 'exiles' who have left their local areas.

Where we are from is thus an important part of our personal identity, and for many of us an important component of this local identity is the way we speak – our accent and dialect. All of us speak with an accent, and all of us speak a dialect. Your accent is the way in which you pronounce English, and since all of us pronounce when we speak, we all have an accent. Some accents, it is true, are more regional than others. There are even a small number of people – probably between 3 and 5 per cent of the population of England – who have a totally regionless accent. This accent is sometimes referred to as a 'BBC accent' because readers of the national news are usually selected from this minority of the population. Similarly, everybody also speaks a dialect. When we talk about dialect we are referring not only to pronunciation but also to the words and grammar that people use. Normally, of course, dialect and accent go together...

What seems to be necessary for someone to change their accent, even if only slightly, is for them to be in frequent face-to-face contact with speakers with different accents. Scots probably hear London accents on television every day of the week, but they do not acquire any features of a London accent unless they move to London and spend large amounts of time talking to Londoners. Television obviously plays a role in influencing the words and phrases people use, but it does not play an important part in influencing their accents or the grammatical structure of their dialects. The point about the television set is that you do not talk to it – and even if you do, it can't hear you...

England seems to be full of people who write to newspapers or the BBC complaining about the way the language is 'degenerating', without appearing to realize that the way they speak and write themselves is the result of thousands of years of language change. They complain about 'Americanisms', and about 'sloppy speech' and 'bad grammar'. The fact is that all dialects are equally grammatical and correct. They differ only in their social significance and function. As a result of a historical accident, the Standard English dialect is today the dialect which is used in writing,

and which, by convention, is used for official purposes. This is why we teach children in British schools to read and write in this dialect. This does not mean, however, that there is anything linguistically inferior about other dialects...

Other forms of English are those that have been brought to England by speakers from countries where English is not a foreign, but a second language. In countries such as India, Pakistan, Bangladesh, Sri Lanka, Ghana, Nigeria, Sierra Leone, Kenya, Tanzania, Singapore, Malta and many others, English is so widely used as the language of education, government and wider communication, that distinctive forms of English have developed. Indian English as spoken by highly educated Indians, has its own characteristic words and pronunciations in the same way that American English does.

Different again are the forms of English, now widely spoken in England, that are of Caribbean origin. Some of these forms are so unlike other forms of English that it would be better in some ways to regard them as languages related to English rather than actually English. These fascinating varieties of language derive most of their vocabulary from English. Many of their grammatical structures, however, stem from African languages and from speakers from all over West Africa who, during the early years of the Atlantic slave trade, had as their only common language a limited amount of English which they fashioned into languages of considerable subtlety and complexity...

In addition to these forms of English, we have to recognise that many English cities are now very multilingual places, with London's schoolchildren in particular, speaking, in addition to English, many scores of different languages as their mother tongue. These languages have come, of course, from overseas in relatively recent times, but England has a long history of being multilingual. In the early years of this century, for instance, very many speakers of the Jewish language, Yiddish, were concentrated in the East End of London. Cornish was spoken in western Cornwall until at least the eighteenth century. And in earlier centuries, refugees speaking Dutch and French fled from religious persecution to England and were present here in many cities in very large numbers. Norwich, to take just one example, was more than one-third Dutch-speaking in the sixteenth century. Very probably, England has not been a monolingual country since the occupation of the originally Welsh-speaking country by the Latin-speaking Romans.

*Adapted from Chapter 1 of **The Dialects of England** by Peter Trudgill (Blackwell, 1990)*

John **Agard**

John Agard was born in Guyana, on the South-American mainland, in 1949. He moved to Britain in 1977, and lives in Lewes, Sussex, with his partner, Grace Nichols.

He has written poetry both for adults and for children. His earlier work is collected in *Mangoes and Bullets*. He has recently published *From the Devil's Pulpit*, a devil's-eye view of the world. In 1998, he was Poet-in-Residence at the BBC.

Half-caste is from John Agard's book of Puffin Teenage Poetry, *Get Back, Pimple!*

John Agard introduces his poetry

I came over to England from Guyana in my late twenties, and I've been living here for just over twenty years. I came over to join my father who had already migrated. In those days, Guyana was called British Guyana – we were a British colony, so freedom of movement was easy...

One of the things I like about England is that you are at the crossroads of cultural connections. Being a Guyanese in England, in a strange way, you become more aware of your Caribbean-ness. People have this idea you're all from 'the Caribbean', but if you're growing up in Guyana you're Guyanese, in Trinidad you're Trinadadian, in Barbados you're Barbadian – and you might never meet someone from St Kitts, or Dominica, or Montserrat. But coming to England, you get that feeling of the Caribbean in a broader way. The diversity of cultures here is very exciting.

It's important to realise that the Caribbean are a people of many textures, shades, colours and cultural connections, with a diversity of voices. Sometimes I write in what you might call 'straight' English, sometimes English inflected with Caribbean creole – it all depends on the poem. Some poems with me come out with a calypso inflection, some maybe like a nursery rhyme – the poem finds its own source. Sometimes I think no punctuation can be effective, because if the words are floating in space, it gives the reader a chance to punctuate with their own breath...

I think humour can be very powerful. There is humour in many spiritual traditions, east and west. You can talk of the sacred clown, the holy fool. Humour breaks down boundaries, it topples our self-importance, it connects people, and because it engages and entertains, it ultimately enlightens. In the Caribbean tradition, calypso uses humour to make powerful, political comments...

Rainbow and *Half-caste*

The rainbow is a source of magic and wonder to any human being, whether you're an English poet or an Aborigine connecting the rainbow to a mythic snake. It's a miraculous thing. You're maybe travelling into London on the Intercity and you see a rainbow over the factories, it fills you with that feeling of wonder. And in my case, because of my Caribbean consciousness, I look at the rainbow and see god doing limbo. It's become a kind of bridge, bridging this culture with other cultures, in a feeling of celebration and joy...

The term 'half-caste' is not one a Caribbean would think of using. Mixed races are part of the Caribbean heritage. My grandfather was from Madeira, my mother is Portuguese but born in Guyana, my father is black. In England, some people very casually use the term 'half-caste' to refer to children of mixed race. And in places like Germany and Holland they speak of 'half-blood', or 'half-breed'. If you take these various expressions together, this imposition of half, half, half on a person's total human complexity implies that some sort of 'purity' has been subverted. A child of mixed race is a tangible, loving expression of human beings from different cultural backgrounds getting together – that should be seen not as something threatening, not something to be paranoid and agonised about, but as something enriching...

Back in the Caribbean, we tended not to refer to 'upper case' and 'lower case', but to 'capital A, common a', 'capital B, common b'. In *Half-caste* the word 'tchaikovsky' has a common 't', 'england' a common 'e', 'picasso' a common 'p' – having it all in lower-case letters, maybe it reduces us all to our common humanity. And poems have a way of taking their own form. You can't dictate that form: it's organic. You can't tell a rosebush not to be a rosebush. *Half-caste* began to come in short lines, I could say like a long shadow being cast, but there's also a long, leaping celebration in the voice of the person – they're leaping into this identity with a sense of joy, and a sense of mischief...

From a BBC television interview, August 1998

Rainbow

When you see
de rainbow
you know
God know
wha he doing –
one big smile
across the sky –
I tell you
God got style
the man got style

When you see
raincloud pass
and de rainbow
make a show
I tell you
is God doing
limbo
the man doing
limbo

But sometimes
you know
when I see
de rainbow
so full of glow
and curving
like she bearing child
I does want know
if God
ain't a woman

If that is so
the woman got style
man she got style

Journey Shango

On new ground we scatter old drum seeds
letting them shape a destiny of sound
unburdening the iron in our blood.
Thunder roots new voice in steel
and lightning seams metal with song.

Who would have dreamed that Shango heart
would beat this far would follow us
across strange water to stranger earth
rising to thunder from oildrum rust?

Listen Mr Oxford Don

Me not no Oxford don
me a simple immigrant
from Clapham Common
I didn't graduate
I immigrate

But listen Mr Oxford don
I'm a man on de run
and a man on de run
is a dangerous one

I ent have no gun
I ent have no knife
but mugging de Queen's English
is the story of my life

I dont need no axe
to split/ up yu syntax
I dont need no hammer
to mash/ up yu grammar

I warning you Mr Oxford don
I'm a wanted man
and a wanted man
is a dangerous one

Dem accuse me of assault
on de Oxford dictionary/
imagine a concise peaceful man like me/
dem want me serve time
for inciting rhyme to riot
but I tekking it quiet
down here in Clapham Common

I'm not a violent man Mr Oxford don
I only armed wit mih human breath
but human breath
is a dangerous weapon

So mek dem send one big word after me
I ent serving no jail sentence
I slashing suffix in self-defence
I bashing future wit present tense
and if necessary

I making de Queen's English accessory/
to my offence

NOTES
Journey Shango
Shango: Caribbean god of thunder, associated with
carnival (see page 38)
Listen Mr Oxford Don
Clapham Common: area of south London; the phrase
'the man on the Clapham bus' is used to signify the
ordinary citizen.
Queen's English: 'standard' English

Half-caste: film treatment

Excuse me
standing on one leg
I'm half-caste

Explain yuself
wha yu mean
when yu say half-caste
yu mean when picasso
mix red an green
is a half-caste canvas/
explain yuself
wha yu mean
when yu say half-caste
yu mean when light an shadow
mix in de sky
is a half-caste weather/
well in dat case
england weather
nearly always half-caste
in fact some o dem cloud
half-caste till dem overcast
so spiteful dem dont want de sun pass
ah rass/
explain yuself
wha yu mean
when yu say half-caste
yu mean tchaikovsky
sit down at dah piano
an mix a black key
wid a white key
is a half-caste symphony/

Explain yuself
wha yu mean
Ah listening to yu wid de keen
half of mih ear
Ah lookin at yu wid de keen
half of mih eye
and when I'm introduced to yu
I'm sure you'll understand
why I offer yu half-a-hand
an when I sleep at night
I close half-a-eye
consequently when I dream
I dream half-a-dream
an when moon begin to glow
I half-caste human being
cast half-a-shadow
but yu must come back tomorrow

wid de whole of yu eye
an de whole of yu ear
an de whole of yu mind

an I will tell yu
de other half
of my story

1 *John (divided image). Somewhere out of vision a mobile of little men swings in the light – it casts distorted shadows on the walls and on his face.*

2 *John's face.*
3 *Flash cuts of paint hitting canvas…*

4 *Light moves to reveal painter using blue and yellow on canvas.*

5 *Painting shots suddenly appear on a monitor, in b&w – we are not sure yet where this is.*
6 *John's face.*
7 *Mobile shadows are cast on the painting and the painter.*

8 *Time-lapse clouds – on the monitor in the foreground. John in b/g – moving light reveals him. We track past monitor.*

9 *Mobile shadow passes over John.*

10 *John's face.*
11 *CU of painting – bright colours.*
12 *John.*

13 *Pan along piano keys*
14 *Painter sits at piano.*

15 *Painter paints the keys of the piano all one colour.*

16 *John.*

17 *Shadow of mobile over side of painter's face.*

18 *Splashes of paint hit the floor and change colour – these are on the monitor. John in b/g.*
19 *Holds out hand as if to shake.*
20 *A hand appears on the monitor – they don't connect. John in b/g of shot.*

21 *CU mobile shadow passes across the crypt wall. The camera pans with it to reveal a still picture of the painted piano.*
22 *John out of focus in b/g.*

23 *The painter casts a coloured shadow on the floor.*

24 *John's face in series of fractional screen images.*

25 *The mobile is revealed – it is made out of four black and four white cardboard cut-outs of men. They all cast the same shadows on the wall.*
26 *Painter paints the camera lens – it goes black. Camera pulls back to reveal it is on the monitor. John exits in b/g.*

Half-caste: exploring the text

(i) Read what John Agard says about himself and his poetry on page 22. Are there interesting connections between what he says here and the poem, *Half-caste*, either in terms of the way the poem is written, or in terms of what it is about?

(ii) The 'tone' of a poem reflects the poet's attitude both to the reader and to the subject matter of the poem. Listen to John Agard's peformance of *Half-caste*, either on the broadcast programme, or on the audio tape. Does his reading help you to understand the tone in which the poem is written?

(iii) Read the other poems by John Agard on page 23. Can you see any similarities between the poem, *Listen Mr Oxford Don* and *Half-caste*? For example:

- the person to whom each poem is addressed
- the style of humour and word play used
- the underlying beliefs which the poems suggest.

(iv) The title of *Journey Shango* refers to the same god who appears in Grace Nichols' poem, *Hurricane Hits England* (page 40). It is one of a set of poems called *Man to Pan*, celebrating the spirit of the West Indian steel band. What does this poem suggest about cultural continuity?

(v) The draft film treatment for this poem (page 24) uses images in a particularly adventurous way – it's not just a literal account of the text. Does it work?

- Watch the broadcast version of this poem. Has it more or less followed the draft treatment published in this book? What changes do you notice?

- Are there points in the film at which the viewer is likely to be surprised, or even confused, by the sequence of images? Is that a bad thing?

- Is there anything in the style of the filming which matches the style of the writing, or the style of John Agard's performance of the poem?

Suggested writing tasks

1 *Half-caste*

How does the way this poem is written help the reader to imagine the way in which it is to be spoken?

2 *Half-caste* and *Unrelated Incidents*
    by Tom Leonard

Both poems use non-standard forms of English. What does this mean for the voice and style of these poems, and how does this relate to what these poems are about?

3 *Half-caste* and *Presents from my aunts in Pakistan*
    by Moniza Alvi

The speakers in these two poems are both born of mixed marriages – 'half-caste', and 'half English'. Write about the different ways in which the poets explore what this means to them.

Moniza **Alvi**

Born in Pakistan in 1954, Moniza Alvi moved to England as a very young child. She has worked as an English teacher in London. *Presents from Pakistan* is from Moniza Alvi's first collection, *The Country at My Shoulder*. A second collection, *A Bowl of Warm Air*, appeared in 1996. She revisited Pakistan for the first time in 1993.

Moniza Alvi introduces her work

I was born in Lahore, in Pakistan, in 1954. My father is from Pakistan originally, and my mother's English – they met when my father was in England on an apprenticeship. They went back to Pakistan, but eventually decided to return to England. I came here when I was a few months old, to Hatfield in Hertfordshire.

I never actually learned my father's language, which I've always been a bit sad about. But I think it sometimes happens that if it's the father's language, contact with fathers often being a bit more remote, it's not always passed on.

Growing up, I felt that my origins were invisible, because there weren't many people to identify with in Hatfield at that time of a mixed race background or, indeed, from any other race, so I felt there was a bit of a blank drawn over that. Although as a child, of course, I was quite happy to be thought of as just the same as everybody else. I was brought up in the Church of England. My father's religion is Muslim, but he wasn't a practising Muslim. I think I had a fairly typically English 1950s/60s upbringing. Then I went to York University, and after that a teacher training course in London – I've taught for twenty years in London schools. I didn't revisit Pakistan until 1993.

Maybe I don't consider anywhere as entirely home, and that's an effect of having been born in a different country, and having some connections with it. When I eventually went to Pakistan, I certainly didn't feel that was home – I'd never felt so English. And also my father seemed very English there, which surprised me. But I never feel entirely at home in England, and of course, I'm not part of the Asian community at all. And it feels a bit odd sometimes that because of the group of poems that I've written about my Asian background, I sometimes tend to be identified as a black writer. I tend to think of England as being very culturally mixed now.

I suppose I would define identity very broadly in terms of what you do, what you respect, and maybe something deeper, your spirit. But it's important to know where you come from, which is perhaps what I was lacking as a child. I think it's important to know what has gone into your making, even quite far back, I think it gives you a sense perhaps of richness. And I found it was important to write the Pakistan poems because I was getting in touch with my background. And maybe there's a bit of a message behind the poems about something I went through, that I want to maybe open a few doors if possible.

I'm attracted by the visual: I think that's quite a strong thing in the poetry. And I always read my poems aloud to myself a lot while I'm writing them, and afterwards. Looking back you can sometimes feel that something is very much in your own voice, or maybe hasn't worked so well because it's not. I feel that the poems in the *Presents from Pakistan* section in *The Country at my Shoulder* are probably quite strongly in my voice. I suppose I found a subject there that was very much my subject, and I think that helps. For example, say, having a baby's very special to you, but it's also very special in somewhat similar ways to everybody else. Maybe I felt I had something here that I hadn't really read about, and that felt particular to me, and that fired me.

Presents from my aunts was one of the first poems I wrote – when I wrote this poem, I hadn't actually been back to Pakistan. It's fairly true, it's fairly autobiographical. The girl in the poem would be me at about thirteen. The clothes seem to stick to her in an uncomfortable way, a bit like a kind of false skin, and she thinks things aren't straightforward for her. It did start off written in blocks in conventional stanzas like big bricks, but I felt it needed to look more lively, and also that it had a lot of individual images which I wanted to give more individual weight to, and I thought this was a way of doing it. It seems to go a bit all over the place and perhaps that's how she's feeling, a bit disoriented.

From a recorded BBC telephone interview, London, June 1998

The Sari

Inside my mother
I peered through a glass porthole.
The world beyond was hot and brown.

They were all looking in on me –
Father, Grandmother,
the cook's boy, the sweeper-girl,
the bullock with the sharp
shoulderblades,
the local politicians.

My English grandmother
took a telescope
and gazed across continents.

All the people unravelled a sari.
It stretched from Lahore to Hyderabad,
wavered across the Arabian Sea,
shot through with stars,
fluttering with sparrows and quails.
They threaded it with roads,
undulations of land.

Eventually
they wrapped and wrapped me in it
whispering *Your body is your country*.

Throwing out my Father's Dictionary

Words grow shoots in the bin
with the eggshells and rotting fruit.
It's years since the back fell off
to reveal paper edged with toffee-glue.
The preface is stained – a cloud rises
towards the use of the swung dash.

My father's signature is centre page,
arching letters underlined – I see him
rifling through his second language.

I retrieve it.
It smells of tarragon – my father's
dictionary, not quite finished with.

I have my own, weightier
with thousands of recent entries
arranged for me – like *chador*
and *sick building syndrome*
in the new wider pages.
I daren't inscribe my name.

An Unknown Girl

In the evening bazaar
studded with neon
an unknown girl
is hennaing my hand.
She squeezes a wet brown line
from a nozzle.
She is icing my hand,
which she steadies with hers
on her satin-peach knee.
In the evening bazaar
for a few rupees
an unknown girl
is hennaing my hand.
As a little air catches
my shadow-stitched kameez
a peacock spreads its lines
across my palm.
Colours leave the street
float up in balloons.
Dummies in shop-fronts
tilt and stare
with their Western perms.
Banners for Miss India 1993,
for curtain cloth
and sofa cloth
canopy me.
I have new brown veins.
In the evening bazaar
very deftly
an unknown girl
is hennaing my hand.
I am clinging
to these firm peacock lines
like people who cling
to the sides of a train.
Now the furious streets
are hushed.
I'll scrape off
the dry brown lines
before I sleep,
reveal soft as a snail trail
the amber bird beneath.
It will fade in a week.
When India appears and reappears
I'll lean across a country
with my hands outstretched
longing for the unknown girl
in the neon bazaar.

NOTES
The Sari
Hyderabad: city in central India
**Throwing out my
Father's Dictionary**
swung dash (~): form of abbreviation
used in dictionaries
chador: shawl worn in northern India
An Unknown Girl
henna: natural dye used for body
painting
kameez: loose top, tunic

Presents from my aunts in Pakistan: film treatment

They sent me a salwar kameez
          peacock-blue,
               and another
      glistening like an orange split open,

embossed slippers, gold and black
          points curling.
      Candy-striped glass bangles
          snapped, drew blood.

      Like at school, fashions changed
          in Pakistan –
the salwar bottoms were broad and stiff,
          then narrow.
My aunts chose an apple-green sari,
      silver-bordered
          for my teens.

tried each satin-silken top –
      was alien in the sitting-room.
I could never be as lovely
          as those clothes –
      I longed
for denim and corduroy.
      My costume clung to me
          and I was aflame,
I couldn't rise up out of its fire,
      half-English,
          unlike Aunt Jamila.

I wanted my parents' camel-skin lamp –
      switching it on in my bedroom,
to consider the cruelty
      and the transformation
from camel to shade,
      marvel at the colours
          like stained glass.
My mother cherished her jewellery –
      Indian gold, dangling, filigree.
          But it was stolen from our car.
The presents were radiant in my wardrobe.
      My aunts requested cardigans
          from Marks and Spencers.

My salwar kameez
      didn't impress the schoolfriend
who sat on my bed, asked to see

1 *Interior: bedroom. Two girls – one Asian, one white in denim skirt. They are giggling as they unpack the presents.*

2 *Asian girl looks in mirror – full length with chamfered edges to give distorting area – when she tries clothes on, golden sunlight floods the room.*

3 *A beam of light hits the slippers as she moves towards the dressing table, drops bangle.*

4 *Slow-motion as bangle breaks on table surface.*

5 *Camera moves to reveal reflection in photo of her in apple-green sari…*

6 *…pull focus to photo – her in blue salwar. Images superimposed.*

7 *…adult wipes frame to reveal her in lounge.*

8 *…track into her, adults wipe pass the foreground, an echoey buzz of conversation – she looks miserable. Lounge net curtains blow in background.*

9 *Friend in denim skirt wipes through frame to reveal we are now back in the bedroom.*

10 *Seen in mirror – her friend holding costumes against herself. Girl in orange salwar looks on, at skirt…*

11 *…red/gold blur… image of girl – shoot this through multicoloured glass-beaded curtain.*

12 *Mix through to…*

13 *Lamp – turned on, it is now evening. Track out to see…*

14 *…her sitting on her parents' bed – colours light her face*

15 *In one of the segments of the lamp, a camel briefly appears like a mirage.*

16 *Glittering, out of focus jewellery, held up to the light.*
17 *Mix to reflection in car window – thief attacks it.*
18 *Granules of glass hit the road, bouncing like jewels.*
19 *Mix to move from behind sparkling clothes – Asian girl hangs clothes up.*

20 *Friend laughs as she flops back on the bed.*

my weekend clothes.
But often I admired the mirror-work,
    tried to glimpse myself
        in the miniature
glass circles, recall the story
    how the three of us
        sailed to England.
Prickly heat had me screaming on the way.
    I ended up in a cot
in my English grandmother's dining-room,
    found myself alone,
        playing with a tin boat.
I pictured my birthplace
    from fifties' photographs.
        When I was older
there was conflict, a fractured land
    throbbing through newsprint.
Sometimes I saw Lahore –
        my aunts in shaded rooms,
screened from male visitors,
    sorting presents,
        wrapping them in tissue.

Or there were beggars, sweeper-girls
    and I was there
        of no fixed nationality,
staring through fretwork
        at the Shalimar Gardens.

21   *Asian girl holds up mirrored garment – reflections in the small mirrors cast highlights on her face.*

22   *Mix to photograph of the three figures on a ship. This picture is in the lounge, by the net-curtained window. (They are the sort with large holes in them – like fretwork.)*

23   *Girl picks up the picture – we hear echoey screaming.*

24   *CU picture – like a mirage it changes to a shadowy live-action shot of a little girl playing with a boat. Water reflections sparkle the little girl's face.*

25   *Net curtain blows across lens to reveal old picture of Lahore...*

26   *...and again... a newspaper cutting?*

27   *...camera tracks from behind the net curtain – we see the aunts. They are wrapping the presents to her, similar to the ones we saw earlier.*

28   *They hold white tissue paper to lens, like net curtains...*

29   *...mix to dust in the air to reveal sweeper girls in the Shalimar gardens...*

30   *...mix to fretwork-like net curtain – wiping to reveal the same shot as a photo in the lounge.*

NOTES
salwar kameez: loose trousers and tunic, traditionally worn by Pakistani women.
Lahore: poet's birthplace in Pakistan (see page 26)
Shalimar Gardens: ornamental park in Lahore

'What you wear speaks volumes about who you are'

The image on the right appeared on a 1998 promotional postcard for the clothing company, La Redoute. The slogan on the reverse side of the card reads: 'Distinctively French, defiantly different, La Redoute'

What you wear speaks volumes about who you are

Resource text

'You are what you wear'

The image here is an advertisement for ChenOne clothing of Lahore which appeared in a 1998 edition of Libas International, an 'exotic fashion and life-style magazine', targeted at English-speaking Asian female readers.

Presents from my aunts in Pakistan: exploring the text

(i) Read Moniza Alvi's account of her background on page 26. As she explains, the girl in the poem is herself as a young teenager in the 1960s. Does she say anything about her life which helps you to understand the experiences described in *Presents from my aunts in Pakistan*?

(ii) The other Moniza Alvi poems included here (page 25), also deal with personal experiences and with the idea of cultural identity.

- In *The Sari*, the poet imagines her own birth in Pakistan. What is the significance of the sari in this poem? In what sense is 'your body your country'?

- In *Throwing Out My Father's Dictionary*, the poet reflects on the different experiences of first and second generation immigrants. What does the image of the dictionary mean to her in this context?

- Moniza Alvi wrote *An Unknown Girl* during her first return visit to Pakistan in 1993. What do you think made the experience described here a memorable one for her?

(iii) Look at the two advertisements on pages 29 and 30. The main slogans in the two texts are similar. What do these advertisements suggest about young people's attitudes to clothing, and how might this be related to Moniza Alvi's poem?

(iv) Read the draft treatment on page 28-9, then watch the programme's film version of *Presents from my aunts in Pakistan*.

- Are there differences from the original script? Why do you think these changes have been made?

- Which images in the film make the strongest impression on you? Which lines in the poem seem to you the most important in understanding how the girl feels? Do the images in the film and the images in the poem work in similar ways?

- The poem deals with the two sides of someone's identity. The film makes use of a number of different kinds of *transition* to move from one image to another (see page 10). How does the editing of the film reflect the experiences described in the poem?

Suggested writing tasks

1 *Presents from my aunts in Pakistan*

How does the speaker in this poem feel about the presents she receives? Refer in detail to the wording of the poem.

2 *Presents from my aunts in Pakistan* and *Hurricane Hits England* by Grace Nichols

The speakers in both poems are living in England, but have been reminded in different ways of the other countries in which they were born. How does the sense of exile come across in these poems? Is this tension resolved in the poems' endings?

3 *Presents from my aunts in Pakistan* and *Half-caste* by John Agard

The speakers in these two poems are both from mixed marriages – 'half English' and 'half-caste'. Write about the different ways in which the poets explore what this means to them.

Kamau **Brathwaite**

Edward Brathwaite was born in 1930 at Bridgetown, Barbados, then the most 'English' of West Indian islands, from where he won a scholarship to Cambridge University, to study history. From 1955, he worked for seven years in Ghana, as an Education Officer, returning to the West Indies in 1962. 'I had, at that moment of return, completed the triangular trade of my historical origins. West Africa had given me a sense of place, of belonging... And I came home to find I had not really left. That it was still Africa, Africa in the Caribbean.'

The Kikuyu name 'Kamau' was given to Brathwaite in a naming ceremony in Kenya in 1971, and used by him as an additional forename until 1987, when he changed his name by deed-poll to Kamau Brathwaite.

Brathwaite has combined his work as a poet with his work as a teacher and academic historian, and his involvement in the Caribbean Artists' Movement. Since 1963, he has taught in the History Department of the University of the West Indies, Jamaica, and more recently at the University of New York, where he is visiting Professor of Caribbean History.

Brathwaite's first three books of poetry, *Rights of Passage* (1967), *Masks* (1968) and *Islands* (1969), together make up what was later published as *The Arrivants: A New World Trilogy* (1973). The trilogy is a work of reconnection, both personal and historical – the reclamation of identity for West Indian people through an exploration of their roots in the African past. A second 'Bajan' (Barbadian) trilogy – *Mother Poem* (1977), *Sun Poem* (1982) and *X/Self* (1987) – continues this personal/historical exploration in a more directly autobiographical way. Brathwaite's later work (for example, *Middle Passages*, 1992) is notable for its degree of technical experiment, in typography and form, and in the poetics of West Indian creole, or what Brathwaite calls 'nation-language'. *History of the Voice* (1984) is his account of the development of this language in West Indian poetry.

Ogun is from the *Possession* section of the book *Islands*, first published in 1969. Brathwaite has commented on this poem, and the memories which surround it, in the memoire-anthology *Barabajan Poems* (Savacou North, Jamaica, 1994).

Kamau Brathwaite has recently returned to Barbados, where he is re-working his second trilogy, first published during the 1970s and 80s.

Kamau Brathwaite introduces his work

What kind of childhood do you remember?

I was brought up on Brown's beach, which is right on the sea. My first memory is seeing the light of the sea reflected on the walls of my room. Then, my father's people were in what we called the country, in the sugar cane area. So I was brought up fishing and bathing in the sea, and then going to the country and being with people who cut sugar cane and drove lorries with sugar cane on... Since I came back here to Barbados, I've noticed that tourism has taken over the beaches, so the Barbadians are being pushed inland.

Is Barbados still 'home'?

The thing for me is the continuity. My father's sisters are still alive, aged ninety, and they still live in the same house that I was brought up in, in Mile&Quarter. Until recently the island was very much as I remembered it for so many years – to return here is to re-affirm essential links.

Could you talk about your own sense of identity as a Caribbean writer?

Identity in the Caribbean is a complex and plural business. You're an islander, you're a little Englander, but you are also in the closest spot in the Americas to Africa. The educational system teaches you almost exclusively about England, but your folk, your street, your yard, your mother's milk, connect you with the Africa across the horizon. As you begin to write you search for something which is not so beholden to others, you begin to walk your beaches, you begin to try to name or re-name your trees, you begin to enter into a kind of subterranean exploration of who you are, what is the nature of your 'I' – 'I' as a pronoun, and 'EYE'. And you begin to get a sense that you, yourself, and your people and your culture are much more complex than you had assumed.

You changed your own name at some point, didn't you? Was that the reason?

When I went to Kenya in the seventies, the people there asked me, why do I have a name like Edward, what does it mean? I couldn't even say what it meant. I just said it had been given me by my parents. So they said they would like to give me an African name, which they did, as Kamau. You see this is another identity struggle here, because the instinct of people both overseas and in the Caribbean, when they have a choice between the use of Edward or Kamau, is to go for Edward, though my preference is Kamau.

What does the word 'culture' mean to you?

Your culture is the world you live in, and the way you define the world you live in. For instance, the original Caribbean people were Amerindians. Then, of course, there is the European settlement of the archipelago, and the African and the East Indian. So we have this notion of a plural culture – but out of that plural culture, you've got to find your own orientation, and not to let it be divisive, but to allow it to teach you as much as it can of your background and your own history and ancestry. You know, like, why do we dance in that way, why do we prefer certain kinds of food? And then, of course, how do the cultures not only come together but live together. Because as long as you are no longer self-conscious and uncertain about your own culture, it is a delight really to relate and share with other people.

That's why I love teaching, which is part of my personality, and part of my writing – what I like about the job each time is the sharing, the learning from the students. And in New York it's exciting because you have a multicultural and multiracial situation where you are able to demonstrate that people do share things, and that the notion of racial prejudice is something that is really, you know, quite ridiculous. I teach Caribbean literature, but any literature is a basis for understanding.

How important to you is this sense of your own cultural history?

If you're going to be an artist, you need to have roots. If you're going to write a story, if you're going to have a sense of myth and legend, all of these things which come out of dreams – they do have a source, they do come from somewhere, and the clearer the somewhere they come from is, the more confident your writing and expression becomes. I've always wanted to give my poetry a very strong sense of its origin.

Is your poetry mainly autobiographical?

My poetry deals with the excavation of the Caribbean psyche. There are my individual memories, but as my poetry started to develop, I heard not only my voice but I began to hear the voices of a crowd of witnesses. It is always in my case 'we' rather than 'I'.

Who is 'we'?

Well, in my case, it was my ancestors. My poetry started as answering the question, how did we get here, and why are we in the condition that we're in? And in my imagination, having lived in Africa as well, I saw a whole coffle of people coming out of the Sahara into the forests of West Africa, and across the Atlantic, into the Americas, and then spreading out from there into all the other parts of the world. So it was that 'we' of the diaspora, the scatteration of people, that I was concerned with. I mean in *Islands* what I was saying was, OK, here we are in the Caribbean, why is it that Africa is still so absent, so that *Islands* is looking for gods who are just barely visible.

So as I began to write, I began to discover my culture. Things that I didn't know I knew, I began to know, and that is really what is so exciting about it, the self-discovery through metaphor of self and of community. Then I discovered I needed to do research, and the two things began to mesh – the research into Caribbean history and discovery of information through metaphor.

Is *Ogun* that sort of poem?

It's about my grandfather's brother, Robert O'Neill – known as Bob'ob. It's about a skilled carpenter who carries within himself the memory of Africa. He has to go into his shuttered Sunday shop, to retreat into himself in order to pursue this knowledge of Africa. So the poem is not only the celebration of a relative, a craftsperson, but the exploration of the notion of continuity, the kind of writing we were talking about, the link between Africa and the Caribbean, and a rare individual, eccentric, whatever you want to call him, who did more than just dream of it, but who tried in his quiet way to realise it, within his own art and craft.

Extracts from recorded BBC telephone interview, Barbados, June 1998

The winds from Africa

in december to about april every year, a drought visits the islands... this dryness, unexplained, is put down to 'lack of rain'.

but living in st lucia at this time, i watched this drought drift in towards the island, moving in across the ocean from the east... and i suddenly realised that what i was witnessing – that milky haze, that sense of dryness – was something i had seen and felt before in ghana. it was the seasonal dust-cloud, drifting out of the great ocean of sahara – the harmattan. by an obscure miracle or connection, this arab's nomad wind, cracker of fante wood a thousand miles away, did not die on the sea-shore of west africa, its continental limit; it drifted on, reaching the new world archipelago to create our drought, imposing an african season on the caribbean sea. and it was on these winds too, and in this season, that the slave ships came from guinea, bearing my ancestors to this other land...

*Brathwaite: Sleeve note to **Rights of Passage** LP (1968)*

OGOUN

My uncle made chairs, tables, balanced doors on, dug out
coffins, smoothing the white wood out

with plane and quick sandpaper until
it shine like his short-sighted glasses.

The knuckles of his hands were sil–
ver knobs of nails hit, hurt and flat–

tened out with blast of heavy hammer. He was knock-knee'd, flat-
footed and his clip clop sandals slapped across the concrete

flooring of his little shop where canefield mulemen and a fleet
of Bedford lorry drivers drop in to scratch themselves and talk

There was no shock of wood, no beam
of light mahogany his saw teeth couldn't handle

when shaping squares for locks, a key hole
care tapped rat tat tat upon the handle

of his humpbacked chisel. Cold
world of wood caught fire as he whittle: rec-

tangle window frames, the intersec-

ting **X**

of fold–
ing chairs, tri–

angle trellises, the donkey box–
cart in its squeak–
ing square

But he was poor and most days he was hungry
imported cabinets with mirrors, formica table
tops, spine-curving chairs made up of tubes, with hollow
steel-like bird bones that sat on rubber ploughs,

thin beds, stretched not on boards, but blue high-tension cables,
was what the world preferred

And yet he had a block of wood that would have baffle them

With knife and gimlet care he worked away at this on Sundays

explored its knotted hurts, cutting his way
along its yellow whorls until his hands could feel

how it had swelled and shivered, breathing air,
its weathered green burning to rings of time,

its contoured grain still tuned to roots and water.
And as he cut, he heard the creak of forests:

green lizard faces gulped, grey memories with moth
eyes watched him from their shadows, soft

liquid tendrils leaked among the flowers
and a black rigid thunder he had never heard within his hammer

come stomping up the trunks. And as he work within his shattered
Sunday shop, the wood take shape: dry shuttered

eyes, slack anciently everted lips, flat
ruin face, eaten by pox, ravaged by rat

and woodworm, dry cistern mouth, crack
gullet crying for the desert, the heavy black

enduring jaw: lost pain, lost iron:
emerging woodwork image of his hunger

This is how Ogun appears in *Barabajan Poems* (Savacou North,
New York, 1994), a book of personal reminiscences interspersed
with a selection of Brathwaite's poems.
  In the same work, he writes about his current interest in
typographical layout – what he calls his 'Sycorax video' style:

The video style comes out of the resources
locked within the computer, esp my Mac's Sycorax and Stark (but not peculiar to
them or me) in the same way that a sculptor like Bob'ob or Kapo wd say that the
images they make dream for them from the block of the wood in their chisel

When I discover that the computer cd write in light, as X/Self tells his
mother in that first letter he writes on a computer, I discovered a whole new way of
SEEING things I was SAYING So that the video is the nearest I can get to what the
athlete or the dancer or the actor says

Besides the forces that created the computer are very similar to the gods
of the Middle Passage, so that the more I go into 'video', the more I become
engaged with the same kind of cosmological/pebbular interfaces, if you like, that a
'simple carpenter' like my Uncle Ogoun was involved in

And it results in new says, new forms and that can't be a bad thing

Milkweed

1

But my father has gone out on the plantation
he used to make us windmills
spinnakers of trash when the crack of cane was in the air

the brown stalks wrinkled and curled in the wind like
scarecrows of orange angels
and butterflies flickered as the clipped straw clicked
on its pin as it picked up speed

but for years he brought us nothing
for years he has told us nothing
his verbs shut tight on his briar

while my mother watches him go
with his cap and his limp and his skillet of soup
and we never look at his hands

2

look at his hands:
cactus cracked, pricked,
worn smooth by the hoe,
limestone soil's colour:
he has lost three fingers
of his left hand falling
asleep at the mill:
the black crushing grin
of the iron tooth'd ratchets
grinding the farley hill cane
have eaten him lame
and no one is to blame

the crunched bone was juicy
to the iron: there was no difference
between his knuckle joints
and ratoon shoots: the soil
receives the liquor with cool flutes:
three fingers are not even worth
a stick of cane: the blood
mix does not show, the star-
gaze crystal sugar shines
no brighter for the cripple blow:
and nothing more to show
for thirty years' spine

curving labour in clear
rain, glass-eyed, coming off
the sea, fattening up the mud
in the valleys, cours-
ing down hillsides, caus-
ing the toil of the deep,
well-laid roots, gripping soil,
to come steadily loose, junction and joint
between shoot and its flower to be made nonsense
of:
and the shame, the shame, the shame-
lessness of it all, the name-
less days in the burnt cane-
fields without love; crack of its
loud trash, spinn-
ing ashes; wrack
of salt odour that will not free
his throat: the cutlass falling, fall-
ing: sweat, grit between fingers,
chigga hatching its sweet nest
of pain in his toe
and now this and now this:
an old man, prickled to sleep by the weather, his
labour,
losing his hands...

NOTES
chigga: a flea that lays its eggs beneath human skin

Ogun: exploring the text

(i) Read the text of *Ogun* published in the NEAB anthology.

- How does the poet build up a sense of his uncle's working life in the first twenty lines of the poem?

- The word 'but' (line 20) and the words 'and yet' (line 27) seem to signal points of development in the argument of the poem. What contrasts are being drawn here?

- The second half of the poem (from line 27 onwards) is different in several ways from the first. How has the imagery changed? Is there a change in the style in which the poem is written?

- How would you interpret the 'anger' of the last line?

(ii) Watch the broadcast film version of *Ogun*.

- How does the film convey the nature of the carpenter's working world? What part does the soundtrack of the film play here?

- How does the film respond to the shift in style and viewpoint in the second half of the poem?

(iii) Read the information on page 38 about Yoruban gods, particularly Ogun. You could argue that the title of this poem refers to the carved image which the uncle creates, or to the uncle himself. Which do you think is more likely?

(iv) To understand the full significance of this poem, you need to know something about the history of the Caribbean people. Read the interview on pages 32-3, in which Kamau Brathwaite talks about this history, and his personal exploration of it. Does this affect the way you interpret or respond to the poem?

(v) What connections can you make between *Ogun* and *Milkweed*, the poem printed on page 34?

(vi) Brathwaite is a habitual re-writer of his own published work. The second part of *Milkweed*, for example, had already been published in a slightly

different form as *Labourer* in earlier books. The version of *Ogun* which Brathwaite reads on the broadcast programme is different both from the original (1969) version published in the NEAB anthology, and the version included here, published in 1993.

- Listen carefully to Kamau Brathwaite's reading of *Ogun*, on the television programme or on the accompanying audio tape. What differences do you hear from the text in the anthology? How might you explain these differences?

- Read the note on page 36 in which Brathwaite writes about his interest in typography. What changes from the original text can you see in the version on pages 35-6?

- Is the change of font significant here? What other 'presentational devices' might you comment on?

- One word changes completely in this version. How does that change affect the poem's meaning?

Suggested writing tasks

1 *Ogun*

The carpenter in *Ogun* leads a double life – his working week and Sundays. Write about the differences between the two worlds and how these are brought out in the way the poem is written.

2 *Ogun* and *Hurricane Hits England* by Grace Nichols

Both these Caribbean poets, Kamau Brathwaite and Grace Nichols, make reference in their poems to an African religion. Explain why this is important to them, and how it shapes the meaning of each poem.

3 *Ogun* and *Search for my Tongue* by Sujata Bhatt

In both these poems, the poet writes about a search for something. What, in each case, does the search involve, and are there similarities in the two situations?

Resource text

Yoruban gods

The faith of the Yoruba people of Western Nigeria was transported to the Americas in the slave ships during the seventeenth, eighteenth and nineteenth centuries. In the Caribbean, the worship of African gods such as Shango or Legba was for many years prohibited by the authorities, but survived in underground forms which varied across the slave cultures of the Caribbean islands, South America and the Southern States.

The phenomenon of possession, in which worshippers may take on the characteristics of a god during the course of a religious ceremony, is central to Yoruban and other African faiths. The carving of images to use as masks or in the construction of altars is an important aspect of the African artistic and religious heritage. The Yoruba people hold their ancestors in great respect, since they believe that the dead are in contact with their gods.

Shango: the thunder god

Thunder gods are found almost everywhere in West Africa, as in many other parts of the world. The powerful tornadoes, which yet bring the longed-for rain, make the spirits of the storm important in the life of the people: thunder, lightning, thunderbolt, and rainbow. In the forests of the Ivory coast there are many storm spirits which have different names. Here, as in many other places, it is held that the thunder god brandishes an axe which he casts to the earth on occasions... I have in my possession a wooden axe, with wooden symbolical double blades, belonging to the Yoruban god Shango, and it is decorated with faces looking in four directions and two others looking forward and backward, like the Roman god Janus...

From E.G. Parrinder, **West African Religion** *(1961)*

Ogun: Lord of Iron

Vitality is the key to the many aspects of Ogun. He is the mighty lord of iron and god of metals, and operator of the divine forge. Since he is the creator of tools, he is known as the father of technology. Ogun is also the god of war, and is himself a powerful and tireless warrior. Furthermore, he is credited with bringing civilisation: when the gods first came to earth their path was obstructed by dense shrubbery, but Ogun with his machete cut quickly through this obstacle. Ogun is synonymous with justice: in Nigerian courts of law an individual may swear upon a piece of iron (representing Ogun) instead of the Bible or the Koran. Ogun also symbolises the place he is said to inhabit and that is the forest. He is the archetypal 'green man' or 'wild man of the woods', and the woods themselves. For this reason, Ogun shrines are often located outdoors, at the roots of sacred trees. The forced migration of the middle passage is perhaps the most important explanation for the multiple incarnations of the Ogun spirit throughout the Caribbean.

By Jane Steele, from the website of **Oshùn***, a periodical for students of ancient African traditions at* www.tiac.net/users/bpantry/voodoo/legba.htm

Oya: she who rides the wind

'Oya is the Yoruban goddess of the wind. She's a very powerful goddess. She was the second of Shango's three wives, but she was also at one time the wife of Ogun, the god of iron. She ran off with Shango, having stolen Ogun's weapons. She's very unpredictable – she doesn't stay in one place. She represents the idea of something that is more felt than seen. So her major symbol is the mask – because you can't really see the face of the wind. And it's said that she's such a terrible goddess that no-one wants to see her face. She's also a symbol of regeneration and newness – another of her symbols is the broom that sweeps clean, gets rid of all the rubbish, all the negativity. So she represents sweeping change. When you have a hurricane, so much is destroyed – cities, fields – you have to start again.'

Grace Nichols speaking in interview about Oya

Grace **Nichols**

Grace Nichols was born in Georgetown, Guyana in 1950. She worked in Guyana as a teacher and as a journalist before moving to England in 1977. She now lives in Sussex with her partner, John Agard. Her first book of poems, *i is a long memoried woman*, won the Commonwealth Poetry Prize in 1983. She has since published three further volumes of poetry and several book for children.

Grace Nichols introduces her work

I grew up in a small country village along the Atlantic coast, in Guyana. As a child, I remember being able to spend long stretches of time by myself, running around in the open, or playing with my friends – we had a freedom which a child growing up in England doesn't have.

And it was a more communal way of life – we related to a much wider circle of people. My grandmother lived with us, cousins and so on, visiting all the time. My younger daughter, Kalera, is growing up like a little English child – she leads much more of an indoor life than I led when I was growing up in a village in Guyana, looking at television, reading. And nowadays, children mature more quickly – we had a longer childhood.

Guyana is a former British colony, so that link was there. We grew up being familiar with English culture. I grew up reading 'William' books, Enid Blyton, then when I was older, Jane Austen, Shakespeare, Keats, so in a strange kind of way I was already familiar with England, even before coming. Of course, when you come in person the differences hit you – the people are different, the climate is different.

But there are lots of things about England which I like. I like the sense of anonymity that I get here – nobody bothers you too much, the way you dress, the way you look. In Guyana, people are more interested in your business, people visit you a lot – whereas in England, I get more time to be on my own. Culturally, England is very rich in terms of theatre, which I love, art galleries, bookshops – I like that very much about England. London, especially, is still kind of exciting for me.

I feel at home now both in Guyana and in England. When I'm in Guyana, or another part of the Caribbean (because I see myself as coming from the wider Caribbean also), I feel I belong there because I spring from that landscape. I'm still enriched by the myths and the legends and the landscape. But partly because I have children in England, I also feel at home in this culture, with their dreams and aspirations. So I embrace both. England is

where I live, where I make my living, but when I'm in England, I'm always looking back. Both as a writer and as an individual, I'm always looking at both worlds.

I live by the sea at Lewes, near Brighton. I often go down to the sea just to clear my head – I love walking along beside it, especially when it's very wild. It's that endless repetition, endlessly folding and rippling. And the universality of the sea, the same motion, the same wave coming in.

Hurricane Hits England was inspired by the actual hurricane that occurred in England in 1987. I remember lying in bed during the Great Storm and feeling all the effects of the hurricane – the sound of the wind rattling the windows, the lightning – the power went off at one stage. The next morning, as I walked around Lewes, especially in the parks, I was very moved by the sight of all the trees that had come down. They seemed to be like so many creatures, like beached whales. My mind couldn't help going back to the Guyana rainforest, so I made that connection with my own Guyana landscape, and with the Caribbean hurricane.

It seemed as though the voices of the old gods were in the wind, within the Sussex wind. And for the first time, I felt close to the English landscape in a way that I hadn't earlier. It was as if the Caribbean had come to England.

Sea Timeless Song

Hurricane come
and hurricane go
but sea... sea timeless
sea timeless
sea timeless
sea timeless
sea timeless

Hibiscus bloom
then dry-whither so
but sea... sea timeless
sea timeless
sea timeless
sea timeless
sea timeless

Tourist come
and tourist go
but sea... sea timeless
sea timeless
sea timeless
sea timeless
sea timeless

Hurricane Hits England

It took a hurricane, to bring her closer
To the landscape
Half the night she lay awake,
The howling ship of the wind,
Its gathering rage,
Like some dark ancestral spectre,
Fearful and reassuring:

Talk to me Huracan
Talk to me Oya
Talk to me Shango
And Hattie,
My sweeping, back-home cousin.

Tell me why you visit
An English coast?
What is the meaning
Of old tongues
Reaping havoc
In new places?

The blinding illumination,
Even as you short-
Circuit us
Into further darkness?

What is the meaning of trees
Falling heavy as whales
Their crusted roots
Their cratered graves?

O why is my heart unchained?

Tropical Oya of the Weather,
I am aligning myself to you,
I am following the movement of your winds,
I am riding the mystery of your storm.

Ah, sweet mystery;
Come to break the frozen lake in me,
Shaking the foundations of the very trees within me,
Come to let me know
That the earth is the earth is the earth.

Island Man

(for a Caribbean island man in London who still wakes up to the sound of the sea)

Morning
and island man wakes up
to the sound of blue surf
in his head
the steady breaking and wombing

wild seabirds
and fishermen pushing out to sea
the sun surfacing defiantly
from the east
of his small emerald island
he always comes back   groggily groggily

Comes back to sands
of a grey metallic soar
                        to surge of wheels
to dull North Circular roar

muffling muffling
his crumpled pillow waves
island man heaves himself

Another London day

We New World Blacks

The timbre
in our voice
betrays us
however far
we've been

whatever tongue
we speak
the old ghost
asserts itself
in dusky echoes

like driftwood
traces

and in spite of
ourselves
we know the way
back to

the river stone

the little decayed
spirit
of the navel string
hiding in our back garden

NOTES
Huracan: Caribbean god of hurricanes. The Caribbean takes its name from the Carib Indians who were the islands' original inhabitants. 'Hurricane' is an English version of the Carib word.
Shango, Oya: African storm gods (see page 38).
Hattie: the name of a hurricane which struck the Caribbean. Until recently, hurricanes were always identified by female names.

Hurricane Hits England: exploring the text

(i)   Read *Hurricane Hits England* aloud. How does the pattern and rhythm of the poem develop? How did you decide what kind of voice to read it in?

- The hurricane is referred to in various ways in this poem. What seems to you to be the balance of positive and negative connotations? What does this tell you about the poet's response to the storm?

- Does Grace Nichols find an answer to the questions she asks herself during the poem?

(ii) The proper names in this poem are likely to be unfamiliar – in reading the poem, you'll have made some kind of guess at their significance. Look now at the information on page 38 about Yoruban gods and see if this falls into place. What does this bring to the poem?

(iii) Read what Grace Nichols says on page 39 about her own cultural history. Does this help you to enlarge your interpretation of the poem?

(iv) Read the newspaper report, 'Countryside counts the toll of uprooted trees', which appeared in *The Times* the day after the Great Storm (page 42). Both report and poem were written in response to the same experience of devastation, though are evidently very different kinds of text.

- What aspects of the storm are most important to *The Times'* agricultural correspondent? What aspects are most important to Grace Nichols?

- What is different about the way in which the two texts are written? Think about choices of person, tense, vocabulary, sentence structure, tone and reference.

- Would it be possible to carve out a new poem using a selection of words and phrases from the report? Have a go.

(v)   View the film version of this poem.

- What genre of film does this most remind you of? Does that suit the poem?

- What is the impact of the director's choice of lighting and lighting effects in this film?

- Which aspects of the poem cannot be communicated through visual imagery and sound?

(vi) *Island Man* and *We New World Blacks* (page 40) are also poems about migration. What links can you make between these poems and *Hurricane Hits England*? (There is a film version of *Island Man* in the 1996 BBC English File 'Poetry Backpack' programme on Grace Nichols.)

Suggested writing tasks

1   *Hurricane Hits England*

Explain the meaning of Grace Nichols' final line, and show how this idea has developed out of the experience described in the poem as a whole.

2   *Hurricane Hits England* and *Blessing*
    by Imtiaz Dharker

The elements feature strongly in both these poems: how do the poets convey the significance to them of water and sunlight in the one case, and storm in the other?

3   *Hurricane Hits England* and *Charlotte O'Neil's Song*
    by Fiona Farrrell

The speakers in both these poems have chosen to cross an ocean and live somewhere else. How does each feel about the country they have left behind?

Resource text

Countryside counts the toll of uprooted trees

By John Young, Agriculture Correspondent

Hundreds of thousands of trees, many of which will not be replaced for generations, have been uprooted and destroyed by the hurricane-force winds which swept across southern and eastern England on Thursday night.

The devastation is by far the worst that has occurred since the outbreak of Dutch Elm Disease which wiped out about 20 million trees in the late 1960s and 1970s.

A national assessment was impossible yesterday as workmen struggled to clear blocked communications and to forestall further danger from damaged trees and branches.

Claims were pouring in to the headquarters of the National Farmers' Union Mutual Insurance Society in London after farmers throughout the South and East suffered stock losses, damage to buildings and power cuts.

The NFU said that farmhouses, grain stores, barns, livestock units and glasshouses had all been damaged, some seriously, in the hurricane-force winds.

At one poultry unit in Essex, 17,000 birds had been killed or would have to be destroyed. In East Sussex, a tree had fallen across a building containing dairy cow and calf pens.

Grain store roofs were ripped off as far north as Peterborough, Cambridgeshire. Recently harvested crops exposed to the storms which could not be covered by emergency sheeting were also damaged. The power cuts disrupted milking operations and cold stores. Any fruit still left on trees was destroyed.

In the horticultural area of West Sussex, between Worthing and Chichester, whole glasshouses were flattened and damage was provisionally estimated at nearly £3 million.

An NFU official said: 'I have spoken to many farmers and growers, and without exception, they have said they have never known anything like it'.

Some of the worst devastation occurred in the New Forest, where Mr Roger Newlands, the Forestry Commission's operations manager, said that hundreds of trees had been uprooted.

Live electricity power lines entangled in fallen trees and branches were hindering the efforts of about 75 staff who were working to clear roads and damaged trees in the area.

Mr Newlands said: 'It is the worst we can ever remember. We have had storms and heavy snowfalls before, but never anything like this'.

In Kent, the town of Sevenoaks lost six of the trees on which its name rested. The commission offered to replace them with a gift of new saplings.

A spokesman at its Edinburgh headquarters said that damage to Thetford Forest, Norfolk and the area around Woodbridge, Suffolk was also bad. Some areas in Northamptonshire had been evacuated.

He said that it would be Monday at the earliest before a preliminary overall assessment of the losses could be made.

The Countryside Commission said that, beyond the immediate task of clearing up the damage, there would be a long-term loss to the environment. Mature trees could not be replaced quickly. The most vulnerable trees were those with shallow roots, mainly conifers, but some hardwood species, such as beeches and oaks, were also badly affected.

The Council for the Protection of Rural England expressed concern that so many trees were top heavy in terms of age. Older trees were particularly vulnerable to that sort of natural disaster, which highlighted the need for long-term replacement.

Tree surgeons said yesterday that they would be working for six months to clear up and repair fallen and damaged trees after the gales.

Mr Barry Still, of Kingston, south-west London, said he had received 400 emergency calls, including one from a woman whose baby escaped death by a few feet when a tree crashed into a bedroom.

Mr Still spent the afternoon clearing 30 fallen oak trees, all at least 200 years old, from a garden in Warren Road, Kingston, near Coombe Hill Golf Club.

He blamed local councils for the huge number of old oaks and beeches which were uprooted in the area. 'Time and time again the lady who owns these oaks has asked permission to have them pruned and the council has refused because it is a conservation area. If they had not been top heavy, they would still be there.'

Responsibility for clearing roads rests primarily with local authorities, who will also have to bear the cost of the operations.

Responsibility for removing trees and branches on private land which constitute a public hazard rests with the owners.

In the Home Counties, the average cost to householders with fallen trees will be nearly £100, with a large oak costing up to £400. An oak or beech with a thick trunk is worth £200 for the timber, although it will fetch much less because of a glut after the storms.

The Times, 17 October 1987

Imtiaz **Dharker**

Imtiaz Dharker was born in 1954 in Lahore, Pakistan, to a Muslim family. She grew up in Glasgow, where she obtained an MA in English Literature and Philosophy. She now lives in Bombay, India, where she works as an artist and film-maker. Her two books of poetry, *Purdah* (1989) and *Postcards from god* (1994), have recently been published in UK in one volume by Bloodaxe Books, together with the drawings which Dharker has done to accompany them. Purdah explores the condition of Muslim womanhood, and some of the tensions associated with living across cultures. The sequence, *Postcards from god*, written in the wake of the Bombay blasts of 1993, looks at questions of faith and intolerance through the eyes of a carefully lower-cased god.

Imtiaz Dharker introduces her work

Could you tell us something about your background?

I was born in Lahore, in Pakistan, in 1954. I came to Scotland when I was a year old so I don't remember anything of Lahore from that time. I went to school in Glasgow. The school was a very strict girls' school – crepe stockings, hats with pins, box-pleated skirts, it was dreadful. Then Glasgow University.

My father and mother wanted us to have the very best education. At the same time, you know how it is, immigrant family, they did not want me to go out with boys, and I was quite keen to keep my cultural base. I didn't eat pork, I didn't drink, I tried within my own limitations to be a good Muslim, partly because I saw that not in religious terms but in cultural terms, and I saw that as quite important. I did know that I wanted to return to the sub-continent, I thought Pakistan at that time. But what I hadn't bargained for was that I'd meet someone who was an Indian Hindu – and being a Pakistani Muslim this was a serious offence. So I eloped, and went to India.

It was something my parents never accepted, and I didn't see them then for the next ten years. I met my father years later and I had to go up to him and he didn't recognise me. I had to say 'I'm Imtiaz, your daughter'. He does meet us now.

Where do you think of as home?

I live in Bombay, that's the place I live and work in, and the reason I'm in India is because I married an Indian.

And it has become home now. I wasn't sure for a very long time if it was home, but it is now. Though sometimes I feel as if writers don't have homes, that I belong in the cracks between countries, and the spaces left over by other people, and I actually, maybe in some ways, prefer it that way. I don't necessarily want to belong to anyone or anything.

Do you write in any other language than English?

No, I don't. English is really my first language. I would love to write in Urdu, but I think that might be a different kind of poetry, you know. I also speak Punjabi, and Marathi, which is my husband's family language. And French and German.

What does 'identity' mean to you?

For me, my identity has nothing to do with nationality, or religion, or gender. It has to do with beliefs and states of mind. So, for me, identity is not about boundaries and restrictions and rules. I mean I'd like to say that religion, specifically, is not how I would identify myself. I don't think my relation to god has anything to do with the group and the requirements of the group. My attitude to faith is much more personal.

My daughter has always said, I'm half Hindu and half Muslim, and has thrown everyone. She certainly grew up celebrating the Hindu festivals, especially with her Hindu grandmother. Now what we do is celebrate everything. We celebrate Christmas, we celebrate Easter, we celebrate Ganpati and we definitely celebrate anything that involves fun and happiness. We're not interested in the back-beating and the flagellations and the worst excesses of Hinduism taking form in India at the moment.

You've written about the effect religion has on the freedom of women. Could you talk about that?

Every religion has been hijacked by self-seeking politicians, by the brokers of power, and the brokers of power are usually men. Even when it's not men, it's women going along with it all – the grandmother can be a great propagator of the downtrodden role of the women under her power. That's where I hold back very seriously from all organised religion. If any god were to impose the kind of sanctions which are laid down in most of the religions, I wouldn't want to know that god. It's not the god I'm talking to when I pray... There is a great conspiracy to keep women under the thumb of men, and religion has always helped in that. I don't think Christianity has been any kinder than any of the others.

What things are you most interested in writing about?

The narrowing of minds and the opening of minds. Windows opening or not opening, the whole feeling of private spaces and outer spaces, the fragility of what we construct around us, the fragility of the human body and of the structures we use to hold our pride and our sense of ourselves. In Bombay, everything is falling down, every building is held up with sellotape and string, all of India seems to be collapsing. And then, of course, you get from that to the whole question of temples and mosques having been brought down, what happens when people begin to break each others' structures. Those are the things I'm struggling with.

Is there anything that seems to you to give your poems a distinctive style?

My first instrinct when I'm writing and when I'm saying the poems aloud is always to get into a kind of iambic rhythm, so what I begin to do then is to break the rhyme, break the rhythm, break it internally. So I take it very much from spoken rhythms, but at the same time I'm trying to do some bouncing off. I'm really talking about the rhythms of my spoken word, which might be different from the rhythms of someone else's. Somewhere in my mind, there has to be the fact that I did read the Koran five times – the rhythm has to be somewhere in there.

Can I ask you about the drawings that accompany your poems? Are they illustrations to the poems, or are they parallel?

They're parallel. I very carefully say the drawings accompany the poems, but they're free-standing, and the poems have to manage on their own as well. It's like different views of the same terrain.

With me, it really does start with an image, for example, the image of eggs in a wire basket, and around that the ramshackle structures you see in a place like Bombay, and the great miracle of the fact that these eggs are still there in the middle of all this impossible collapsing structure. The drawing happened first in that case – it's a theme drawing to the whole idea of a world that is crumbling and collapsing and about to fall, and the whole question of how does human dignity survive in the middle of all this. The whole *Postcards from god* sequence came from that one image of the eggs in the basket.

What is the particular background of *Blessing*?

The scene is very specifically in the largest slum in Asia, which is Dharavi, on the outskirts of Bombay, where there are millions of little huts. Bombay is the city of dreams, Bombay is where everyone hopes the pavements are lined with gold. They've come from all over India. They are migrants to the city, they come in there for a better life and they're living in conditions which to anyone else would look squalid but to them it really is the hope of a better life.

And because it is not an official living area, there is a shortage of water. Bombay can go to forty degrees or more – when the monsoon eventually comes it is a great release then, of course, all the children will be out, even in the floods they will be out playing. But when a pipe bursts, when a water tanker goes past, there's always a little child running behind the water tanker getting the bits of drips and it's like money, it's like currency. In a hot country, in that kind of climate, it's like a gift. And the children may have been brought up in the city and grown up as migrants, but the mothers will probably remember in the village they've come from they would have to walk miles with pots to get to a well, to the closest water source. So it really is very precious. When the water comes, it's like a god.

From a recorded BBC interview, London, August 1998

44

Blessing

The skin cracks like a pod.
There never is enough water.

Imagine the drip of it,
the small splash, echo
in a tin mug,
the voice of a kindly god.

Sometimes, the sudden rush
of fortune. The municipal pipe bursts,
silver crashes to the ground
and the flow has found
a roar of tongues. From the huts,
a congregation: every man woman
child for streets around
butts in, with pots,
brass, copper, aluminium,
plastic buckets,
frantic hands,

and naked children
screaming in the liquid sun,
their highlights polished to perfection,
flashing light,
as the blessing sings
over their small bones.

After Creation

You would think
after all the trouble of Creation,
that things would know their place.

Forget the Garden and the Fall.
Just take all the ordinary things,
the locks and bolts,
the bits of wood,
pieces of tin and plastic,
scraps of food,
the dogs and children,
bicycle wheels,
jars and pots and pumps,
half-pants on a line,

anti-aircraft guns, policemen's
boots and belts, the calendar
full of gods, gas
cylinders, bars of soap.

I had hoped
these things would
work themselves
into some kind of order.

When I began
it was a simpler world.

Things, perhaps, got out of hand.

A woman's place 1

Mouths must be watched, especially
if you're a woman. A smile
should be stifled with the sari-end.
No one must see your serenity cracked,
even with delight.

If occasionally you need to scream, do it
alone but in front of a mirror
where you can see the strange shape the mouth makes
before you wipe it off.

b l e s s i n g

Living space

There are just not enough
straight lines. That
is the problem.
Nothing is flat
or parallel. Beams
balance crookedly on supports
thrust off the vertical.
Nails clutch at open seams.
The whole structure leans dangerously
towards the miraculous.

Into this rough frame,
someone has squeezed
a living space

and even dared to place
these eggs in a wire basket,
fragile curves of white
hung out over the dark edge
of a slanted universe,
gathering the light
into themselves,
as if they were
the bright, thin walls of faith.

One breath

All it would take
is one slammed door
to make the whole thing
fall. One bottle hurled
against a wall,
to start the hammering
on the heart
and crack
the body's shell.
One sneeze, one cough,
one doubt.

All it would take
is one breath,
no more.

Exile

A parrot knifes
through the sky's bright skin,
a sting of green.
It takes so little
to make the mind bleed
into another country,

a past that you agreed
to leave behind.

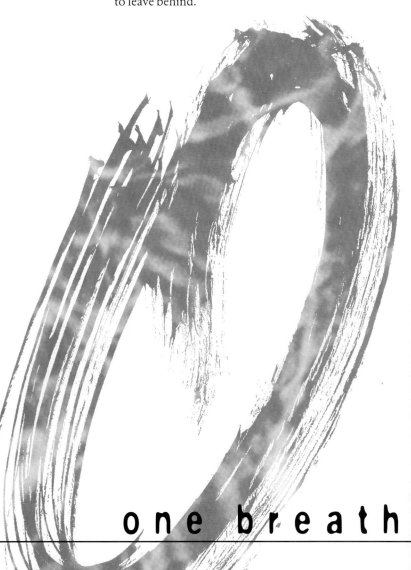

one breath

Blessing: exploring the text

(i) Read the text of *Blessing*. How does the poet control the movement of this poem, line by line? (It may help to listen to the poet's own reading of this poem.)

- How does the poet's choice of words influence the way we respond to this description of a burst water pipe?

- Read what the poet says towards the end of her interview (pages 43-4) about the setting of *Blessing* in Dharavi. Does this help you to get inside the poem?

(ii) You could say that *Blessing* is a 'filmic' poem – vivid, visual imagery and a kind of soundtrack in words. How well does the film version of this poem succeed in capturing these qualities? Which images in the film do you remember most sharply?

(iii) Read the the interview with Imtiaz Dharker on pages 43-4 in which she talks about her personal history and her beliefs. 'I don't necessarily want to belong to anyone or anything', she says at one point. Does the interview help you to understand why she sees things that way? How might the interview illuminate poems like *A Woman's Place* or *Exile* (pages 45 and 46)?

(iv) The poems by Imtiaz Dharker on pages 45 and 46 are from the book, *Postcards from god*, published by Bloodaxe Press. This edition also contains the drawings which she produced to accompany the poems.

- *Living Space* and *One Breath* follow each other in the sequence, and both relate to the drawing of the hanging basket of eggs, which can be seen in the programme. Read the poems aloud to yourself. Read what Imtiaz Dharker says on page 44 about 'fragility'. What do these poems make you most aware of?

- *After Creation* is a poem in which a slightly bewildered god tries to make sense of the world he has created. Are there things about the way this poem is written which remind you of *Blessing*?

(v) Read the advertisement for a holiday tour of India (page 48).

- What impression do you get from this advertisement of the nature of India and its culture? What phrases contribute most strongly to this representation?

- What kind of experience of India would the 'Palace on Wheels' provide?

- What is the effect of reading this advertisement alongside Imtiaz Dharker's poem *Blessing* (or Arun Kolatkar's *An Old Woman*)?

Suggested writing tasks

1   *Blessing*

Why is this poem called *Blessing* and how is this idea developed through the poem?

2   *Blessing* and *An Old Woman* by Arun Kolatkar

What kind of images are created in these two poems, and how did you respond to them?

3   *Blessing* and *Hurricane Hits England* by Grace Nichols

The elements feature strongly in both these poems. How do the poets convey the significance to them of water and sunlight in the one case, and storm in the other?

Resource text

PALACE ON WHEELS

9 DAY INDEPENDENT TOUR
Delhi - Jaipur - Chittorgarh/Udaipur - Ranthambore -
Jaisalmer - Jodhpur - Bharatpur/Agra - Delhi

Tuesday, Day 1

Following your arrival in Delhi transfer to your hotel.

Wednesday, Day 2

The morning sightseeing of Old Delhi is followed by lunch and New Delhi before you arrive at Delhi Cantonment station for the evening reception and board the Palace on Wheels. After dinner aboard the train you will find yourself en route for Jaipur.

Thursday, Day 3

Jaipur is reached amidst much excitement as musicians and caparisoned elephants await at the station to greet you. After breakfast you have a full day's sightseeing in the 'Pink City', breaking for lunch at the stupendous Rambagh Palace, and returning to your carriage in the late evening.

Friday, Day 4

You arrive in Chittorgarh and visit the greatest fort in Rajasthan before leaving by road for the extraordinary oasis town of Udaipur and a full day's sightseeing. Lunch is taken at the exquisite Lake Palace and you return to the train for dinner.

Saturday, Day 6

You pull into Sawai Madhopur and enjoy a morning's sightseeing in Ranthambore National Park, a short drive away. Lunch and dinner are taken on the train as you begin the long haul westwards to Jaisalmer.

Sunday, Day 7

Jaisalmer's crenellated walls rise out of the desert like a mirage.

*A*s the British Raj was quick to appreciate (and travellers to the subcontinent have shown equal enthusiasm), train is the ideal mode of transport in India. Virtually everywhere is accessible by rail, an ever-changing panorama of great vistas and intimate glimpses.

As its name suggests, the Palace on Wheels is no ordinary train but a transport of delight. Just once a week, from September through to April, this palatial hotel on wheels traverses Rajasthan, never covering the same stretch twice in its weekly timetable.

To accommodate the new broad gauge track, the Palace on Wheels has been completely rebuilt from the ground upwards with all modern amenities (such as air-conditioning and private bathrooms with showers) but recreating the ambience and opulence of the original Maharajah's personal coaches upon which these carriages are based. Thus, once aboard, you will find liveried attendants, traditional veneered interiors, ornate ceilings, fully carpeted compartments and corridors in classic Rajput style (all compartments have private bathrooms), restaurant cars with exquisitely tempting menus (both Indian and European cuisines), and a supremely comfortable Bar-Lounge. The Maharajas of old never had it so good.

There is much to do and see here... explore the fort, see the ornate havelis, experience a camel ride on the sand dunes... before returning to the train in the late evening.

Monday, Day 7

The morning will find you in Jodhpur, dominated by the huge Meherangarh Fort. Sightseeing will take place after breakfast with a break for lunch at the colossal Umaid Bhavan Palace, still the royal residence. Dinner is taken on the train.

Tuesday, Day 8

Overnight the train has moved on to Bharatphur renowned for its bird sanctuary. You will have the chance to spot a few rare species before visiting Akbar's abandoned capital of Fatehpur Sikri en route for Agra and lunch at the Mughal Sheraton Hotel. The afternoon is entirely given over to visiting the Taj Mahal and Agra Fort before returning to the train for dinner and the overnight return journey to Delhi.

Wednesday, Day 9

Arrive at Delhi after breakfast and disembark. Our representative will meet you and transfer you to your hotel. The rest of the day at leisure or sightseeing before the late evening drive to the airport for your flight home.

For conditions of travel and full list of tariffs, please refer to the insert.

•HOTELS•

Delhi
Taj Palace (D)

For further hotel classifications see introductory pages

.DELHI
Jaisalmer *Jaipur* *Bharatpur* *Agra*
Sawai
Jodhpur *Madhopur*
Chittorgarh
Udaipur

LAKE PALACE, UDAIPUR

Arun **Kolatkar**

Arun Kolatkar was born in Kolhapur, India, in 1932. He trained first as a painter, then as a graphic artist; he has spent most of his working life as a graphic designer in an advertising agency in Bombay. Kolatkar has published one book of poems in English, an extended sequence called *Jejuri* (1976), which won the Commonwealth poetry prize in 1977. He writes also in the Indian language, Marathi, and has translated his own work from one language to another.

Jejuri describes a pilgrimage or tourist visit to the temple town of that name, near Pune (or Poona), in West Maharashtra, one of the Earth's oldest landscapes. The poems are linked not so much by a narrative thread as by a kind of montage technique: Kolatkar has commented that his first impulse had been to make a movie. *Jejuri* deals playfully with the improbabilities of Hindu legend and beliefs, but also with the mysteriousness of the everyday world. Asked once in an interview if he believed in God, Kolatkar replied 'I leave the question alone. I don't think I have to take a position about God one way or the other.'

Kolatkar did not wish to be interviewed for the BBC programme, though was happy to read his poems aloud, and for others to discuss them. His friend Dilip Chitrie introduces his work below.

Introducing Arun Kolatkar's work

"Arun is a bilingual poet. He writes in Marathi, his mother tongue, and in English, which is everybody's – it's an interesting thing that by the year 2010, the largest number of people using English will be in India, even more than in the United States. Arun is also a bi-cultural person. He has his English language culture and his Marathi language culture, and he fuses these two sources.

If you visit him in his tiny apartment, it's full of books. If he gets interested in something, then he pursues that for a number of years, soaking it up as it were, and it comes out in his work maybe several years later. Arun takes a long time to publish anything. He works on poems sometimes for a number of years – he goes on revising, he has to be sure that he wants to publish.

He puts a great value on his privacy. In Arun's case, it's only his poems that are public – that's the only public face he has. I remember him saying once, 'Criticism is for me a barbed wire fence.' So critics are always beyond the fence. He wants to stay on his own side of it. It's as though he's saying, 'Let my work speak – I won't speak for it.'

Although Arun did not continue as a painter, his painterly eye can be seen in his poems. He wants every image to be absolutely clear – the visual aspect of his poems is often the leading aspect. He works through sound as well, but often the thing that hits you first is a startling image.

Jejuri is about a journey to a place of pilgrimage. In the poem you have sketches of encounters with people, anecdotes, legends. He's looking at the idea of a pilgrimage, though Arun himself is not a pilgrim, he's not a devotee, he's not even a believer. Arun is an urban man, a contemporary man. His poems have a warmth, expressed through humour. He knows the absurdities and the limitations of human nature, and he sympathises with those. The poem is like a journey into his own people's past.

These poems take you to imaginary places. You have to imagine a lot, you have to recreate the place through the words of the poem – so half the contribution has to be from the reader's side, from the reader's imagination."

From a recorded interview with Dilip Chitrie, September 1998.

The Horseshoe Shrine

That nick in the rock
is really a kick in the side of the hill.
It's where a hoof
struck

like a thunderbolt
when Khandoba
with the bride sidesaddle behind him on the blue
horse

jumped across the valley
and the three
went on from there like one
spark

fleeing from flint.
To a home that waited
on the other side of the hill like a hay
stack.

Yeshwant Rao

Are you looking for a god?
I know a good one.
His name is Yeshwant Rao
and he's one of the best.
Look him up
when you are in Jejuri next.

Of course he's only a second class god
and his place is just outside the main temple.
Outside even of the outer wall.
As if he belonged
among the tradesmen and the lepers.

I've known gods
prettier faced
or straighter laced.
Gods who soak you for your gold.
Gods who soak you for your soul.
Gods who make you walk
on a bed of burning coal.
Gods who put a child inside your wife.
Or a knife inside your enemy.
Gods who tell you how to live your life,
double your money
or triple your land holdings.
Gods who can barely suppress a smile
as you crawl a mile for them.
Gods who will see you drown
if you won't buy them a new crown.
And although I'm sure they're all to be praised,
they're either too symmetrical
or too theatrical for my taste.

Yeshwant Rao,
mass of basalt,
bright as any post box,
the shape of protoplasm
or a king size lava pie
thrown against the wall,
without an arm, a leg
or even a single head.

Yeshwant Rao.
He's the god you've got to meet.
If you're short of a limb,
Yeshwant Rao will lend you a hand
and get you back on your feet.

Yeshwant Rao
does nothing spectacular.
He doesn't promise you the earth
or book your seat on the next rocket to heaven.
But if any bones are broken,
you know he'll mend them.
He'll make you whole in your body
and hope your spirit will look after itself.
He is merely a kind of a bone setter.
The only thing is,
as he himself has no heads, hands and feet,
he happens to understand you a little better.

An Old Woman

An old woman grabs
hold of your sleeve
and tags along.

She wants a fifty paise coin.
She says she will take you
to the horseshoe shrine.

You've seen it already.
She hobbles along anyway
and tightens her grip on your shirt.

She won't let you go.
You know how old women are.
They stick to you like a burr.

You turn around and face her
with an air of finality.
You want to end the farce.

When you hear her say,
'What else can an old woman do
on hills as wretched as these?'

You look right at the sky.
Clear through the bullet holes
she has for her eyes.

And as you look on,
the cracks that begin around her eyes
spread beyond her skin.

And the hills crack.
And the temples crack.
And the sky falls

with a plateglass clatter
around the shatter proof crone
who stands alone.

And you are reduced
to so much small change
in her hand.

An Old Woman: film treatment

An old woman grabs
hold of your sleeve
and tags along.

She wants a fifty paise coin.
She says she will take you

to the horseshoe shrine.

You've seen it already.

She hobbles along anyway
and tightens her grip on your shirt.

She won't let you go.
You know how old women are.
They stick to you like a burr.

You turn around and face her
with an air of finality.

You want to end the farce.

When you hear her say,
'What else can an old woman do
on hills as wretched as these?'

You look right at the sky.

Clear through the bullet holes

she has for her eyes.

And as you look on,
the cracks that begin around her eyes
spread beyond her skin.

And the hills crack.
And the temples crack.
And the sky falls

with a plateglass clatter
around the shatter proof crone
who stands alone.

And you are reduced
to so much small change
in her hand.

---

1   *Shot POV – the old woman grabs an arm.*

2   *Flash cut to the same shot in Soho, London at night – a girl beggar grabs an arm.*

3   *Old woman pleads for money, wants to lead him.*

4   *Girl pleads, wants to lead him.*

5   *The shrine*

6   *Cut to Soho neon.*
7   *Pull out to reveal tourist looking at picture of the shrine in his hand – in a London street.*

8   *Bare feet*
10   *Old woman holds onto his shirt.*
12   *Old woman clings*

9   *Flash cut to trainered feet.*
11   *Girl holds onto tourist, obviously enticing him.*
13   *Tight together, the tourist and the girl enter a filthy doorway.*

14   *Tourist turns in anger to old woman.*

15   *Flash cut to same turn in London – tourist turns to girl in a dingy room.*

16   *Tourist holds money out to her, holds it back*

17   *A couple of notes are handed to the girl.*
18   *Girl shrugs.*

19   *Old woman gestures*

20   *Girl gestures to her dingy bed.*

21   *Tourist looks up at sky – it is reflected in his shades. He takes them off and looks down at her.*
23   *Mix to crash zoom out to MCU to match*

22   *Cut to crash zoom from swinging light bulb – it is reflected in his shades, he takes them off and looks down at her… as a shadowy figure looms and hits the tourist from behind.*
24   *CU of his startled eye… crash zoom out to MCU.*
25   *His face slow-mo as he drops.*
27   *His wallet drops, money scatters.*

26   *He tosses coin into bowl, she fumbles – rough begging bowl falls to the ground . Money scatters*
28   *CU money bouncing*

29   *Tourist falls in the dingy room.*

30   *The shards of the bowl bounce around her.*
31   *She looks down*

32   *Girl looks down.*

33   *She scrabbles to pick up the money in the dust.*
35   *Grasps it eagerly.*

34   *She scrabbles for his money.*

36   *Grasps it eagerly.*

An Old Woman: exploring the text

(i)   Read the text of *An Old Woman*.

- There is a 'you' in this poem, but no 'I'. Who do you think 'you' is?

- Where is the turning point in this poem? And what changes?

- What's real and what's unreal in this encounter – or is that the wrong way of looking at it?

- The last five sentences all start with 'And'. What's the effect of that?

- What does the old woman seem to you to represent?

(ii) Read the information on page 49 about Arun Kolatkar and Jejuri – the place itself and the book of poems of that title. Does this help you to appreciate what the poet is doing in this poem?

(iii) Read the draft film treatment for this poem (page 51). When this draft was first submitted, the producer wrote back as follows: "36 shots and 2 days filming to do 65 seconds? Like the idea of parallel stories but there is too much of the London story – the visuals will be so strong that the poem will be lost. Really need to simplify it. No religious aspect? Focus on the eyes – we need to let the emotions come through rather than so much action. And we're going to Jejuri – so we need to see it."

- What do you think of the idea of intercutting two parallel narratives, as a way of responding to this poem?

- What aspects of Kolatkar's poem would you wish to bring out in a film version? Draft an alternative treatment.

- Look at the final broadcast version of this poem. How have the ideas been developed since the original proposal?

(iv) Read *Yeshwant Rao* (page 50).

- How would you describe the tone of the opening few lines?

- What sort of person seems to be speaking in this poem?

- What seems to be the speaker's attitude to the gods listed in verse 3?

- Does Yeshwant Rao fit your idea of a god?

(v)   Read Tatamkhulu Afrika's poem, *The Beggar*, on page 59. What does it have in common with *An Old Woman* and how is it different?

Suggested writing tasks

1   *An Old Woman*

How do you interpret this strange encounter with 'an old woman'? You could write about

- the impression made by the old woman in the first half of the poem

- how the poem changes in its second half

- the implications of the final three lines.

2   *An Old Woman* and *Blessing* by Imtiaz Dharker

What kind of images are created in these two poems, and how did you respond to them?

3   *An Old Woman* and *Nothing's Changed* by Tatamkhulu Afrika

How is the sense of a viewpoint created in each of these poems, and how might that influence the way we respond to the experiences which are described?

Fiona **Farrell**

Fiona Farrell was born on the South Island of New Zealand in 1947, and grew up there, attending Dunedin University. She has lived in England and in Canada, but is now settled back in New Zealand, where she writes plays, novels, short stories and poems. Her first book of poems was *Cutting Out*, published in 1987 (under the name Fiona Farrell Poole). A second book of poems is in preparation.

The musical play, *Passengers*, co-written with Helen Caskie in 1985, and based on research by Charlotte McDonald, features a cast of twenty female working-class migrants on a ship to New Zealand. *Charlotte O'Neil's Song* is one of a sequence of four poems taken from this play, and included in Fiona Farrell's collection, *Cutting Out*.

Fiona Farrell introduces her work

I was born in 1947 in the Otago province of New Zealand. I live now on Banks Peninsula, about an hour and a half from Christchurch, right out in the wilds. I am a New Zealander absolutely. I love the landscape here, I love the emptiness of it.

I suppose I am conscious of having a particular kind of lineage which is important to me. It is important to me for example that my father was Irish and an immigrant, that he came out when he was eight years old. It is important to me that my mother is descended from the Scottish Presbyterians who came out in the 1840s looking for a place where they could practise their religion without interference. And it is important to me that I am part of a culture that is evolving very rapidly – New Zealand is a very questioning and uncertain place at the moment.

I was brought up in an intensely religious household, and by the time I was fifteen, I was heartily sick of established religion altogether. And I think now that the sorts of things that I am writing about are my religion, where I am absorbed by the way in which human beings are part of a wider world, a whole universe, and by the way we connect with other animate and inanimate parts of that.

The Charlotte O'Neil poem comes out of a particular historical situation. The poems I wrote for *Passengers* were written because these people had been forgotten, and that was one of the primary facts about the play. I was asked to write for a cast of twenty young women for a centenary of the YWCA, and a friend was writing a history of immigration in the nineteenth century. In the 1860s, 70s and 80s about 12 000 young women were brought to New Zealand on assisted passages. They were young women, twelve and up, and they were brought out to be servants and to right the gender balance in the colony, to be wives

basically – the government paid for them to come out.

And in the ships' records, there were all these names of young women and where they came from and their employment sometimes, and that was all that we knew about most of them. They simply disappeared into the country, they are very hard to trace. Your name comes down through the male line and often people don't know their grandmother's maiden name, and people don't always keep memories of these things alive, particularly when they move between countries. So the whole point of the play was to give each of the girls in the modern cast a name that had been of someone who had come to New Zealand, and then to try and breathe life into that name again. The research base of the play was diaries and interviews and family stories, so that kind of collective memory was being tapped into.

New Zealand wasn't founded like Australia by convicts, it was actually very deliberately settled. And when they brought out these young women it was to establish a European presence here, and to make the country, what they used to call the Britain of the south. They wanted a European population that would equal and, in fact, outnumber the Maori population – it was part of the whole process of taking over the country. Right now in New Zealand there is an awful lot of re-thinking about what happened in the nineteenth century.

The play is set onboard a ship coming from Britain to New Zealand, down the African coast and across the Southern Indian ocean – most of the ships took about four and a half months to get here. The boats were really very tiny, with very narrow and cramped quarters below decks, and when they came back everything was cleared out, because on the way back they brought timber or something back to Britain.

One of the things that characterised a lot of the people who came out here, and particularly the young women, was that the servants were far too independent, as far as employers were concerned, because they always knew they would be able to find other work. And there were also great opportunities to marry of course, and set up home on their own. And the girl who was acting the part of Charlotte O'Neil in the play was herself a very independent young woman, and as the play developed out of improvisation, Charlotte became quite a stroppy sort of character. When the song was sung in the play, people always applauded at the end of it – they liked the spirit of it, I think.

From a recorded BBC telephone interview, New Zealand, June 1998

Resource text

DAY 83. OFF THE CAPE OF GOOD HOPE

Lights up – a clear day, not blindingly hot. CLARA ROSKRUGE leans on the rail looking out at the first land she has seen for weeks. CHARLOTTE O'NEIL comes up and gives her a book. It's Clara's diary.

CHARLOTTE O'NEIL: You dropped this.

CLARA ROSKRUGE: Oh... thank you.

CHARLOTTE O'NEIL: By the galley.

CLARA ROSKRUGE: I didn't know... thank you.

CHARLOTTE O'NEIL: It's beautiful isn't it? The cape.

CLARA ROSKRUGE: It's land.

CHARLOTTE O'NEIL: See how the sun catches those little houses by the water? *(Pause.)*

CLARA ROSKRUGE: I used to live in a house by the sea. You could hear it always. In winter, it would throw itself at the cliff. My father used to say, 'Devil's stirring it up tonight', and we'd hang on tight to each other, us children, under the blankets. But in summer it was soft as a lamb. *(Pause.)* The rocks here are too big. I don't like them. See. The houses could be crushed in a minute. *(Pause.)* They don't look... permanent. *(Pause.)*

CHARLOTTE O'NEIL: It's the very tip of Africa. One of the ladies on the saloon deck showed me a map this morning. This is just the tip... Behind those rocks there's rivers and jungles and deserts and whole kingdoms. For ever.

CLARA ROSKRUGE: My house was on the tip of England. *(Pause.)* Shall I show you? *(She opens the book.)* There. That's it. My home.

CHARLOTTE O'NEIL: Did you draw that?

CLARA ROSKRUGE: The morning I left. And this is my mother. And these are some leaves from our garden. I've pressed them to remember. This is an apple leaf. And this is clover.

CHARLOTTE O'NEIL: And forget-me-nots. *(Reads.)* 'Though oceans may between us roar, And distant be our lot, Ah though we part to meet no more, Dear friend, forget-me-not.' That's nice.

CLARA ROSKRUGE: Martha gave them to me. A girl I worked with on the farm. *(Pause.)*

CHARLOTTE O'NEIL: Rivers and jungles and deserts. I had no idea it was so far...

CLARA ROSKRUGE: Would you have come? If you'd known.

CHARLOTTE O'NEIL: Yes.

CLARA ROSKRUGE: If you'd known it meant being sick, and cooped up for weeks on end and drinking water that's red from sitting in the sun and...

CHARLOTTE O'NEIL: Yes. I'd have come if I'd known it was twice as far.

CLARA ROSKRUGE: Really?

CHARLOTTE O'NEIL: Do you want to know why? *(Pause – awkward but determined.)* I've never told anyone this. It sounds sort of silly. So you mustn't laugh. *(Pause)* I was scrubbing the steps. I had to clean them every day, early, while the family was having breakfast. they were white steps, five of them. Porch at the top with a mat. Wooden doorstep with brass edgings I polished till I could see my face in them. And there was a metal bootscraper and brush. You had to take the dried mud off that, then sweep and scrub the steps till they were white. They'd be black an hour later of course. But for fifteen minjtes, every morning, they were perfect. I did those steps every day for five years. Ever since I was twelve and went into service. Well, one morning, I was rushing to get done because I hadn't scoured all the pots and Cook would kill me if she knew, and Mrs Fulton came out. She was my employer. Very tall, in a dark blue dress. She had a letter. She stood on the steps I'd just cleaned – they were still wet - and said, 'You're father's died, O'Neil. You can go home when you've finished your work.' Then she went in and shut the door. So I wiped off the marks her feet had made on my steps, and I packed my bag and I went and saw my family. Then I took all my savings and bought my ticket. £3 down. £13 to pay when I get there. And one thing I know, I won't be paying it off scrubbing steps. *(Laughs.)* There. Told you it was silly.

CLARA ROSKRUGE: *(laying a hand on Charlotte's arm)* That's not silly. It's not silly at all...

*Scene from the play, **Passengers**, by Fiona Farrell, with music by Helen Caskie, first performed in 1985.*

Charlotte O'Neil's Song

You rang your bell and I answered.
I polished your parquet floor.
I scraped out your grate
and I washed your plate
and I scrubbed till my hands were raw.

You lay on a silken pillow.
I lay on an attic cot.
That's the way it should be, you said.
That's the poor girl's lot.
You dined at eight
and slept till late.
I emptied your chamber pot.
The rich man earns his castle, you said.
The poor deserve the gate.

But I'll never say 'sir'
or 'thank you ma'am'
and I'll never curtsey more.
You can bake your bread
and make your bed
and answer your own front door.

I've cleaned your plate
and I've cleaned your house
and I've cleaned the clothes you wore.
But now you're on your own, my dear.
I won't be there any more.
And I'll eat when I please
and I'll sleep where I please

and you can open your own front door.

Passengers

Clara Roskruge, 16. Domestic servant. Cornwall.
'Indian Empire' 1864.
Charlotte O'Neil, 17. General servant. Origin
unknown. 'Isabella Hercus' 1871.
Ann James, 33. Laundress. Abergavenny. 'Light
Brigade' 1868.
Harriet Attiwell, 20. Domestic servant.
Leicestershire. 'Cameo' 1859.
Eliza Lambert, 14. Domestic servant. Surrey.
'Mystery' 1858.

Nineteenth-century ships' records

Passengers

Emily Graham, 'Chile', Top of Stafford St,
Common
Amy Graham, 'Chile', Top of Stafford St,
Common
Anne Brown, 'Chile', Pellings Cottages,
Clandestine
Miss Moran, 'Chile', Pellings Cottages,
Clandestine
Miss Parsons, 'Chile', Back of Waverley,
Clandestine

Police records, Dunedin, 1876

Anne Brown's Song

I first spread my legs
on a London street
and the shillings came easy
put shoes on my feet.
(I've lain on clay
and I've lain on sheet . . .)
And men with rough fingers
have staked out their claims
and gone off up country
no addresses no names.
There's gold in my crannies
there's gold in my crack.
Come miners and diggers
I'm down on my back.
There's a crack in the ceiling
a draught at the door
my back aches my mouth's salt
but there's time for one more.

A nice little bar
with a lamp and a chair
and frosted glass windows
to keep out the air
(there's a crack in the ceiling
a draught at the door)
and no man to empty
his load in my box
no fingers no breathing
no crabs and no pox
and I'll pile up the shillings
to keep in the heat
till I lie in the clay
till I lie in the sheet . . .

Charlotte O'Neil's Song: exploring the text

(i) Read the scene from Fiona Farrell's play,
     Passengers (page 54).

 - What can you tell from the way the scene is
   written about the relationship between Charlotte
   and Clare at this point in the play?

 - Do you sense any differences in the
   characterisation of the two girls, and their
   feelings about the decision they have taken?

 - Does Charlotte's long speech help to explain the
   nature of the world she has left behind and the
   feelings she expresses in her song?

 - Would you say her attitude is expressed more
   strongly in the speech from the play, or in the
   song which follows it – and why do you think this?

(ii) Read *Anne Brown's Song*, also from *Passengers*
     (page 55).

 - What can we deduce from the song about the life
   Anne Brown has led?

 - Is she similar in character to Charlotte? Do they
   want the same things?

 - Think about the way the two songs end. How
   would you define the mood in each case?

(iii) On page 53, Fiona Farrell explains some of the
      history behind European immigration into New
      Zealand in the nineteenth century. Does anything
      she says here help you understand the experience
      of young women such as Charlotte O'Neil, Clare
      Roskruge and Anne Brown? In what ways?

(iv) Watch the film version of *Charlotte O'Neil's Song*
     from the programme.

 - What does the film emphasise about Charlotte's
   daily life as a servant?

 - The film mixes images from Charlotte's work
   situation with images of another kind. How does
   the film-maker handle the transitions between
   the two? How does this reflect the way the poem
   is written?

 - Why do you think the director chose a spoken
   soundtrack here rather than a musical one?

Suggested writing tasks

1 *Charlotte O'Neil's Song*

How does the the form of this song reinforce what
Charlotte O'Neil is saying? You might write about

 - the song's rhythm, and its rhyme scheme

 - repetitions

 - contrasting images

2 *Charlotte O'Neil's Song* and *Nothing's Changed*
   by Tatamkhulu Afrika

The speaker in *Charlotte O'Neil's Song* is seventeen.
The speaker in *Nothing's Changed* is much older. How
do the two speakers feel about the past and the future?

3 *Charlotte O'Neil's Song* and *Hurricane Hits England*
   by Grace Nichols

The speakers in both these poems have chosen to
cross an ocean and live somewhere else. How does
each feel about the country they have left behind?

Tatamkhulu **Afrika**

Born in Egypt in 1920, Afrika was fostered in South Africa at an early age. As a young man, he published a novel, *Broken Earth* (Hutchinson, 1940). He fought with the Allies at Tobruk, and was a prisoner of war. He worked for twenty years as a miner in the Namibian copper mines. He is a member of the African National Congress. In 1966 he participated in the uprising against the apartheid government's declaration of Cape Town's District 6 as 'whites only'. Arrested again in 1987 for 'terrorism', he was banned from writing or speaking in public for five years. A widower for many years, he lives in a hut in the Bo-Kaap area of Cape Town. He began writing poetry in his sixties, and has now published five collections of poems documenting his South African experience. *Nothing's Changed* is from Afrika's third book, *Maqabane* ('Comrade'), published in 1994.

Tatamkhulu Afrika introduces his work

I was born in 1920 in Egypt, in a little town called Sulum, on the coast. My father was an Arab and my mother was Turkish, so I'm quite pale in complexion.

My parents came to South Africa when I was about two years old, bringing me with them. And then they died shortly afterwards in a flu epidemic, and I was adopted by friends of theirs, English-speaking South African settlers. And then I had a second set of foster parents later on in life, and they were Afrikaaners.

When I was about to leave school my foster mother came and told me that I was not really their child. She told me about my parents and what they had been, and she said, keep that to yourself, don't spread it around – we've given you our name and we've given you your identity and so on, just keep it.

But when I realised that my origins lay elsewhere, I took a new interest in things Islamic, things Egyptian, and of course during the Second World War we were stationed in Egypt, and the vibes were instant and inescapable – I immediately felt at home. The very smell of the place was known, subconciously known to me, welcomed by me. And when I came back here again after the war, well, I am a South African, my roots may not be here but practically my whole life's experience is here, and I do passionately feel I belong here and would never leave. But there are

times when I would like very much to pay one more visit to Alexandria, Cairo, before I die.

After the war I went up to what is now Namibia, to the copper mines, and I worked there off and on for twenty years. And when I was up there the classification system was introduced down south, but it never was instituted in what was then South West Africa, so when I returned to Cape Town, to District Six, I had no classification. So I applied, like an idiot, and they looked at my photograph and decided I was white. And I said, well I'm not white and I don't want to be white. Shortly after I'd arrived in Cape Town, I'd become a Muslim. My parents obviously had been Muslim, and I wanted to stay in District Six where there were mosques and I could practise my faith. So I refused absolutely to accept the white card.

They pursued me everywhere. To them it was inconceivable that a person who looks white doesn't want to be white. There must be something subversive about me. So that's when I went to Helen Suzman, who was then the lone member of parliament for the Liberals, and she presented the Minister of the Interior with evidence to the effect that I was born an Arab and a Turk. And then I was classified a Malay! And I still have what they call a green card, where I look so incredibly young, with my black Javanese fez on, and these words in the corner, 'Malay' and 'Malaya' in Afrikaans, and I've kept it and I'm going to keep it as a reminder of how insane the world was then.

I had hardly been in District Six for two years when they declared it white, and they started to evacuate us. I was arrested then for the first time because, you know, I've always been a champion of lost causes, much to my sorrow now and again. And I had started a Muslim organisation, Al-Jihad, and already I was writing a little magazine for the organisation. I wrote a scathing article against the government's declaration of District Six as white, and it ended up in the hands of the security police, and I was immediately arrested and had my first taste of what police hands are like.

Then I watched the slow disintegration of District Six, and this to me was a traumatic experience. It left a mark on me which will never go away. You might ask why, after all, I hadn't been there so long. It was because District Six, when I first went into it, had all the vibes of Egypt, it had that smell of poverty, of excrement and urine and poverty, which has a smell all of its own, and spices and incense and so on. I felt so at home. I felt I'd come home at last to a place in this country where I belonged. And then they started to tear it down bit by bit. I'd come home from work in the evenings and another building would have been razed flat by the bulldozers, and the people transplanted to the Cape Flats.

Then in the early eighties, the United Democratic Front was formed, and I was at the inaugural meeting, myself and all my friends, and then eventually the African National Congress emerged into the limelight and we joined the ANC in 1984. And then we started what the authorities would have called terrorist activities, explosives and so on, and we were eventually caught red-handed, and I was sentenced to four years imprisonment. But we had three marvellous advocates – one of them is now the Minister of Justice – and they got the whole sentence suspended.

But the main problem was that I was banned from writing or public speaking for five years, because the charges automatically carried a banning order, so I was unable to write under the name I had then – which was the name of my second foster parents, by deed poll. But then in the ANC, as an undercover agent, I had a code name, and that code name was Tatamkhulu Afrika – so then I wrote under that name, and got away with it. And under this name I feel completely at home, and it's going to be my name until I peg out. I don't think of myself as anything else. It's actually Tatamkhulu Ishmael Afrika, because Ishmael was the name I took as Muslim – I thought well, damn it all, if I'm going to change something, let's change the lot, so I shoved my Muslim name in the middle.

I think of identity as a sort of cloak which surrounds you, like environment. I've been brought up among South African people, particularly black people, who I love most of all, which also becomes part of my identity. I think identity comes from experience. And then it does in a way also come from realisation, mental realisation, like in my case, of what you could have been, like an out-and-out Egyptian.

But I am completely African. I am a citizen of Africa, I'm a son of Africa, I am actually African. That's why we have an element in the ANC which they call 'Africanist'. It's not racial. I feel that if you were born in Africa, you should assimilate Africa. So that is my culture. I know I write poems that sound European, because I was brought up in school to do that, but if you look at my poems carefully you will find that all of them, I think, have an African flavour.

Nothing's Changed is entirely autobiographical. It was after District Six had been dead for a good many years, and I can't quite remember when I wrote this but I think it must have been about eight years ago. District Six was a complete waste by then, and I hadn't been passing through it for a long time. But nothing has changed. Not only District Six... I mean we may have a new constitution, we may have on the face of it a beautiful democracy, but the racism in this country is absolutely redolent. We try to pretend to the world that it does not exist, but it most certainly does, all day long, every day, shocking and saddening and terrible. It's mostly on the white side you know, it's mostly so, although it is on the black side also.

Look, I don't want to sound like a prophet of doom, because I don't feel like that at all. I am full of hope. But I won't see it in my lifetime. It's going to take a long time. I mean, in America, it's taken all this time and it's still not gone... So it will change. But not quickly, not quickly at all.

From a recorded BBC telephone interview, Cape Town, South Africa, June 1998

The Beggar

When I passed
the bus-stop, his black
as biltong hand
thrust out,
demanding alms.
Beneath the grime,
he was a yellow man,
and small,
and crumpled as a towel,
eyes receding into bone,
shivering, too thin frame
denying the truculence of the hand.
"No", I said,
and walked on,
annoyed that I was annoyed,
swatting off shame
all the way into town.
Coming back,
the day-long drizzle stopped
and a suddenly clear
sky sang
of summer round the bend,
white sails in the Bay,
birds grown garrulous again.
I looked for him.
He was lying on his back in the sun,
eyes closed,
stretched out long as a spill,
hardly distinguishable
from any of the other
drifts of debris in the lane.
"Drunk again", I thought,
and paused, then pressed
my penance into his palm.
Quick as a trap,
his fingers lashed
over it: surprised
sober eyes blessed
me for being kind.
Then he slept again,
fist wrapped, tight,
about the bribe my guilt refused,
limbs thrown wide
as though a car had flung him there
and left him to a healing of the sun.

Nothing's Changed

Small round hard stones click
under my heels,
seeding grasses thrust
bearded seeds
into trouser cuffs, cans,
trodden on, crunch
in tall, purple-flowering,
amiable weeds.

District Six.
No board says it is:
but my feet know,
and my hands,
and the skin about my bones,
and the soft labouring of my lungs,
and the hot, white, inwards turning
anger of my eyes.

Brash with glass,
name flaring like a flag,
it squats
in the grass and weeds,
incipient Port Jackson trees:
new, up-market, haute cuisine,
guard at the gatepost,
whites only inn.

No sign says it is:
but we know where we belong.
I press my nose
to the clear panes, know,
before I see them, there will be
crushed ice white glass,
linen falls,
the single rose.

Down the road,
working man's cafe sells
bunny chows.
Take it with you, eat
it at a plastic table's top,
wipe your fingers on your jeans,
spit a little on the floor:
it's in the bone.

I back from the glass,
boy again,
leaving small mean 0
of small, mean mouth.
Hands burn
for a stone, a bomb,
to shiver down the glass.
Nothing's changed.

NOTES

Nothing's Changed
District Six: Cape Town's
'District 6', formerly a thriving
Cape Coloured comunity, was
subject to enforced evacuation
and destruction during the
sixties and seventies, as part of
the then government's policy
of apartheid (see pages 57-8)
Port Jackson trees: imported from
Australia for use on housing
projects; widespread in the
Cape, pushing out the
indigenous trees.
bunny chow: bread stuffed with
pilchards or similar; poor
man's hamburger

Resource text

District Six

District Six is the name of an urban district of Cape Town on the slopes of Table Mountain, which holds a particular significance for South Africans, and especially for the Cape's extensive 'coloured' population.

The early history of the district was bound up with the abolition of the slave trade in 1838. Many of those liberated were Muslims who had been forcibly transported to South Africa from the East Indies by Dutch settlers. Later in the nineteenth century, a boom in the South African mining industry brought rapid growth to the city of Cape Town, which took in Jewish immigrants from Lithuania, plus Dutch and English mineworkers and traders from around the world.

District Six became a prosperous city quarter, built mainly in the English Victorian style, with a mixture of gabled Dutch houses and eastern mosques. It consisted of a busy network of streets around a main thoroughfare, Hanover Street, with a variety of places of worship, markets, schools, shops, neighbourhood parks, cinemas, bath-houses and eating places. Because of its history and location, it had developed into an unusually mixed community, close to the centre of Cape Town, but with its own character and sense of local identity. It contained a notable mixture of social classes, both labourers and professionals. Even more unusually, there was a strong, local tradition of racial and religious tolerance, which meant that black and white, Christian and Muslim, Jew and Hindu, lived alongside each other and shared the full range of local facilities.

By the 1950s, District Six was becoming increasingly overcrowded. It was also attracting the attention of a Boer government now firmly committed to a policy of 'apartheid', or racial segregation. This policy drew a categorical distinction between Black, White, and Coloured (defined as Arab, Asian or mixed-race), and allocated each racial group its own separate residential areas. In 1966, under the new Group Areas Act, President P.W. Botha declared that District Six would henceforth become an area for whites only.

There followed a programme of 'slum clearance' in which all inhabitants who were not registered as white were made to leave their homes, to be rehoused a few miles to the east on Cape Flats. Some 70 000 mainly coloured residents, some with a history of tenure going back over a hundred years, were uprooted as part of a programme of what might now be termed 'ethnic cleansing'. In this upheaval, the sense of a living community which had developed over many years was entirely destroyed. Cape Flats is now a vast expanse of impoverished, dilapidated housing, notorious for its street crime, as rival drug gangs fight for control of the territory.

Following the clearances, the architectural fabric of District Six was razed to the ground, as if to destroy the evidence that such a community had ever existed. The bulldozing was also intended to provide building sites for upmarket residential and commercial property in the new whites-only district, which was officially re-named Zonnebloem ('Sunflower'). But the area has never been properly redeveloped. Of the original buildings, only a few scattered mosques and churches still remain. As the system of apartheid has crumbled, so the ruined townscape of the old district has become a kind of memorial to the cruelty and injustice of an earlier phase of South African history.

Nothing's Changed: exploring the text

(i) Read *Nothing's Changed* (page 59).

- How does the opening verse of the poem 'establish' the scene? What viewpoint does the poem offer us?

- How does the second verse draw us further into the poem?

- How does the poet 'know where we belong'?

- What makes him think himself 'a boy again'?

- What tone of voice would you need to read this poem aloud? What tells you this? Would the tone change between verses?

(ii) Page 60 provides a short history of District Six, and will help to explain the experiences which lie behind the poem. Having read this, do any of the lines in the poem take on an added significance for you?

(iii) Afrika's life-story, which he retells on pages 57-8, gives us a vivid insight into the nature of the regime under which he has lived most of his life. What strikes you most, from this story, about the nature of the 'apartheid' system?

(iv) Afrika says in his interview that he wrote this poem in about 1990 during the period of liberalisation which saw the release of Nelson Mandela, soon to become president of the new South Africa. Read what Afrika says towards the end of his interview (page 58) about his hopes for the future of his country. Does this effect the way you interpret the ending of the poem?

(v) Watch the film version of this poem. The film was shot, with Afrika's assistance, in the locations which gave rise to the experiences described in the poem.

- Is this the kind of landscape you imagined for this poem?

- In what ways does the film manage to convey the interplay of past and present in the poem?

- The film uses reflections in a number of ways. How does this relate to the language and structure of the poem?

- How would you have ended this film?

(vi) Read *The Beggar* (page 59). Write a 'film treatment' for this poem (see the examples on pages 24, 28-9, 51), which responds to the images, narrative structure and feelings in this poem.

Suggested writing tasks

1   *Nothing's Changed*

How does the poet communicate a sense of injustice in *Nothing's Changed*? You could write about

- the historical background, and how this is woven into the poem

- the contrasted images in the poem

- the emotions felt by the speaker, and the way in which these are expressed.

2   *Nothing's Changed* and *An Old Woman* by Arun Kolatkar

How is the sense of a viewpoint created in each of these poems, and how might that influence the way we respond to the experiences which are described?

3   *Nothing's Changed* and *Charlotte O'Neil's Song* by Fiona Farrell

The speaker in *Charlotte O'Neil's Song* is seventeen. The speaker in *Nothing's Changed* is much older. How do the two speakers feel about the past and the future?

Specimen questions

NEAB GCSE English Paper 2
Poems from Other Cultures and Traditions

1   Choose two poems which deal in some way with the experience of moving between different cultures, and explain in each case how this is reflected in the imagery of the poems.

2   Choose two poems which communicate a sense of injustice, and show how the poet has succeeded in doing this.

3   Choose two poems which make connections between the past and the present, and show what this means to the writer.

4   Show how any two of these poets explore the idea of cultural identity in the poems you have studied.

5   Compare two poems from different cultures which seem to you to have something in common, and explain why you think this is so.

6   Write about two poems in which the form and style of the writing seem to you particularly effective.

7   How is the sense of exile explored in two of the poems you have studied?

8   Explain how a knowledge of the cultural context has helped you to interpret and respond to any two of the poems in this selection.

9   Choose two poems in which the titles seem to you to pin-point what the poems are about, and explain in each case how this idea is developed in the course of the poem.

10   Choose two poems in which the final line seems to you particularly important. Show in each case how the poem builds towards this conclusion.

11   Choose two poems which deal with an experience of inner conflict or confusion, and show how this is developed through the language and imagery of the poems.

(See also the questions on specific pairs of poems elsewhere in the 'Exploring the text' sections of this book.)

Suggested media assignments

NEAB GCSE English Coursework

1   Choose one of the film versions of these poems, and show in detail how the film-maker has used the resources of film to reflect aspects of the poem.

2   Compare the film interpretations of any two of these poems, and explain which seems to you to be the more successful. Refer in detail to the ways in which both films have been made.

Assessment objectives: NEAB GCSE English

Reading: Paper 2, Section A

What you write in the examination is marked according to assessment objectives which are listed
in the syllabus. The following objectives apply to both the poetry questions on Paper 2.

The first three objectives are do with your ability to understand the question, and to plan and organise an answer. *(You will need to spend a few minutes sorting out your thoughts before you start writing.)*	
1 'select material appropriate to the purpose'	• Can you focus clearly on the wording of the question and select two poems to write about which are relevant to it?
2 'make appropriate reference to texts'	• Can you refer closely to the poems you have chosen, quoting words or phrases, or mentioning line numbers?
3 'make cross references'	• Can you make connections between the two poems you have chosen, including any direct points of comparison or contrast?
The next three objectives are to do with your ability to read the poems with understanding, and to explain what you think they are about, and how you respond to the poet's ideas and feelings.	
4 'follow an argument'	• Can you show how the meaning develops through the course of the poems? Can you explain what each poet is thinking and feeling at the end of the poem, and how this relates to what has gone before?
5 'read with insight and engagement'	• Can you show insight into the writer's attitude in each poem, and into the experiences with which the poems deal? Can you explain your personal response to the poems?
6 'develop and sustain interpretations of texts'	• Can you refer closely to details in the two poems in order to explain what you think each poem is about? Can you explain things which are left implicit in the poem? Do you understand something about the cultural contexts from which the poems come?
The last three are to do with your ability to see how the poems have been written, and how the poets' choice of structure or wording contributes to the meaning and effect of the poems.	
7 'understand and evaluate linguistic devices'	• Can you explain why certain words and images have been chosen by the poets, and how sound and connotation contribute to the impact and resonance of a poem?
8 'understand and evaluate structural and presentational devices'	• Can you draw attention to how the poems are shaped and patterned on the page, and how this contributes to their meaning? Can you make a personal judgement on how effectively the poems have been crafted?
9 'comment on ways language varies'	• Can you comment on the ways language and style varies between the poems, showing some awareness of the distinctive voice of each writer and how this has been created?

For further ideas in relation to the last three assessment objectives, see 'Thinking about Poetry' on pages 4-7.

Select bibiliography

Sujata Bhatt

Brunizem (Carcanet, 1988)
Monkey Shadows (Carcanet, 1991)
The Stinking Rose (Carcanet, 1995)

Tom Leon ard

Intimate Voices: Selected Work 1965-1983 (Galloping Dog
1988; Vintage 1996)
Reports from the Present: Selected Work 1982-94
(Jonathan Cape, 1995)
Norah's Place & other poems 1965-1995
(AK Press Audio: CD AKA006)

John Agard

Mangoes and Bullets: selected and new poems 1972-84
(Pluto Press, 1985)
Get Back, Pimple! (Viking, 1996)
From the Devil's Pulpit (Bloodaxe, 1997)

Moniza Alvi

The Country at my Shoulder (Oxford University Press, 1993)
A Bowl of Warm Air (Oxford University Press, 1996)

Kamau Brathwaite

The Arrivants: A New World Trilogy,
(Oxford University Press, 1973)
Mother Poem (1977), *Sun Poem* (1982) and *X/Self* (1987)
– the 'Bajan' trilogy (Oxford University Press)
Middle Passages (Bloodaxe, 1992)
DreamStories (Longman Caribbean Writers, 1994)
Black + Blues (1976, reissued/revised New
Directions 1995)

Grace Nichols

i is a long memoried woman (Karnak House, 1983)
The Fat Black Woman's Poems (Virago, 1984)
Lazy Thoughts of a Lazy Woman (Virago, 1989)
Sunris (Virago, 1996)

Imtiaz Dharker

Postcards from god (Bloodaxe, 1997)

Arun Kolatkar

Jejuri (Clearing House, Bombay, 1976)

Fiona Farrell

Cutting Out, (Aukland University Press,
New Zealand, 1987)

Tatamkhulu Afrika

Dark Rider (Snail Press/Mayibuye, South Africa, 1992)
Maqabane (Mayibuye Books, South Africa, 1994)
Turning Points (Mayibuye Books, South Africa, 1997)

Acknowledgements

With thanks to the *Roots and Water* production team:
Producer: Jacqui Doughty; Director: Clive Wagner; Camera: Matt Gray;
Researcher: Natasha Soma

Every effort has been made to trace the copyright holders of material used
in this book. If, however, any omissions have been made, we would be
happy to rectify this at the earliest opportunity.

Sujata Bhatt for *Search for my Tongue* and *A Different History* from *Brunizem*,
published by Carcanet Press Ltd., *At the Flower Market* from *Monkey
Shadows*, published by Carcanet Press Ltd., *The Voices* from *The Stinking
Rose*, published by Carcanet Press Ltd.; Tom Leonard for biographical
information and for *Poetry, Unrelated Incidents 2 and 3, A Summer's Day* and
Fathers and Sons from *Intimate Voices: Selected Works 1965-83*, published by
Vintage, *Situations Theoretical and Contemporary* and *A Handy Form* from
Reports from the Present (©Tom Leonard), published by Random House UK
Ltd.; John Agard for *Half-caste* and *Rainbow* from *Get Back Pimple*,
published by Viking, *Listen Mr Oxford Don* and *Journey Shango* from
Mangoes and Bullets, published by Pluto; Moniza Alvi for *Presents for my
aunts in Pakistan, The Sari, Throwing out my Father's Dictionary* from *The
Country at my Shoulder,* published by Oxford University Press, *An Unknown
Girl* from *A Bowl of Warm Air*, published by Oxford University Press;
Kamau Brathwaite for sleeve note to *Rights of Passage* LP, *Ogun*, extract from
Barabajan Poems, published by Savacou North, New York, and *Milkweed*
from *Mother Poem*, published by Oxford University Press; Grace Nichols
for *Sea Timeless Song, Island Man* and *We New World Blacks* from *Fat Black
Women's Poems*, published by Virago Press, *Hurricane Hits England* from
Sunris, published by Virago Press; Imtiaz Dharker for *Blessing, Living Space,
One Breath, Exile, A Woman's Place 1* and *After Creation* from *Postcards from
god*, published by Bloodaxe Books; Arun Kolatkar for *The Horseshoe
Shrine, Yeshwant Rao* and *An Old Woman* from *Jejuri*, published by Clearing
House, Bombay; Fiona Farrell for *Passengers*, and for *Charlotte O'Neil's Song*
and *Anne Brown's Song* from *Cutting Out*, published by Auckland University
Press; Tatamkhulu Afrika for *Nothing's Changed* and *The Beggar* from
Maqabane; Peter Trudgill for extract from *The Dialects of England*, published
by Blackwell; La Redoute advertisement created in-house by La Redoute
design team S. Sutcliffe and J. Crawford (page 29); Chen One
advertisement courtesy of Libas International (page 30); E. G. Parrinder for
extract from *West African Religion*, published by Epworth Press (page 38);
Oshún website for extract by Jane Steele (page 38); *The Times* for article
from *The Times*, 17 October 1987 (page 42); Palace on Wheels
advertisement courtesy of Greaves Travel (page 48).